EDIBLE
SHRUBS

The production of this book has been supported by a grant from Schöck Familien Stiftung gGmbH of Steinbach, Baden-Baden, Germany.

Copyright 2019 by Plants For A Future
First Edition
Plants For A Future is a charitable company limited by guarantee, registered in England and Wales.
Charity No. 1057719, Company No. 3204567
The PFAF website and Plants Database are at pfaf.org
Book Design: PembertonCreative.com
Plants text: Trevor Pemberton
Introductory sections: David Gearing & Chris Marsh

Plants For A Future

General Disclaimer

Each entry includes information on the potential medicinal uses of the various products that can be obtained from the plant, but we do not attempt to define or identify preparations suitable for treating each ailment mentioned.

To the best of our knowledge all the information contained herein is accurate. But of course we cannot guarantee that everyone will react positively to all plants described as edible in this book or to other plant uses suggested herein.

It is commonly known that many people suffer allergic reactions to conventional foods and products. Even amongst the more commonly eaten fruits, for example, there are plenty of instances where people react badly to them:

- Many people are allergic to strawberries and will come out in a rash if they eat them.
- Some people develop a rash if they touch the stems of parsnips.
- Potatoes become poisonous if they turn green.
- Eating large quantities of cabbage can adversely affect the thyroid gland.

We strongly recommend the following precautions when trying anything new:

- Make sure you have identified the plant correctly
- Try a small quantity of anything you have not eaten before. Only increase the quantity consumed once you are satisfied that there are no undesirable side effects.
- When trying new soaps or skin applications try them on a very small area before proceeding to larger areas of the body. Look for any uncomfortable reactions or changes before widening the application.

No liability exists against Plants for a Future or any trustee, employee or contractor of Plants for a Future, nor can they be held responsible for any allergy, illness or injurious effect that any person or animal may suffer as a result of the use of information in this book or through using any of the plants mentioned in it.

Plant Key

♥ Medicinal 🍐 Edible rating. ⚒ Other uses rating
1= minor uses, 2= reasonably useful plants, 3= standard crops, 4= very useful, 5= great value. A subjective evaluation.

🌱 Spring 🌞 Summer 🍂 Autumn ❄ Winter 🌾 Carbon Farming Plant Ⓩ USDA Hardiness Zone

🌊 Water Plant ✕ Dry Soil 💧 Moist Soil 💧 Wet Soil ☀ Full Sun 🌗 Part Shade 🌑 Full Shade 🪴 Plant Size

Edible Plant Part: ❀ Flowers 🍃 Leaves 🌱 Stem 🌿 Root 💧 Oil 🍐 Fruit 🌼 Pollen 🌰 Seed

Hardiness Scales. Information on two hardiness scales are included: the USDA Hardiness scale and the PFAF hardiness scale. The PFAF hardiness scale is a plants hardiness from from 1 - 10. One will survive arctic winters, ten is tropical. Cornwall is about eight, but can grow some plants from zone nine. Most of Britain is zone seven, going down to zone six in the north and four in the mountains. Please see pfaf.org/hardiness/ for more information.

Contents

Foreword

When I first heard that PFAF were embarking on a new book on edible shrubs, I was very excited to discover the list of plants included and also felt the timing couldn't be more crucial. The book introduces 73 shrubs from PFAF's extensive database which are important perennial food crops, as well as having carbon uptake properties. It provides a much-needed launch pad for inspiring small-scale reforesting and sustainable food production, as well as being an invaluable resource and in-depth guide packed with useful information.

If we want to do something about climate change, build local resilience, provide food for ourselves and cultivate crops for the future, the time to act is now. Yes, we can put pressure on our governments, but we can also take direct action. While the wheels of our political system turn slowly and agreements are made for some distant date in the future, there are immediate steps we can take in our own backyards and our communities to effect change. We can become radical gardeners, growers and farmers of a different kind. Whilst the ability of perennial plants to absorb carbon has long been understood, shrubs play an important role in this process. The brilliant thing is that the last time I checked there were no laws against growing shrubs! We don't need permission to start a food forest revolution. By a process of stealth we can begin to re-populate our planet with useful, edible and carbon absorbing plants in small scale systems capable of feeding our communities. We can radically alter our environment and how we produce food - one shrub at a time. The information in this book will show you how to do exactly that.

I have been an activist my whole life, a journey which has taken me into the world of growing and researching perennial vegetables and useful edibles. I founded Incredible Vegetables to learn more about perennial food crops and set up a small nursery to supply some of the plants I was most excited about. This is not only my passion but something I feel utterly compelled to do, as the work has great significance for the future. I have created a perennial 'food glade' and am proud to say that it includes the majority of the plants listed in PFAF *Edible Perennials* book, with the aid of which I now share my findings with others and am slowly amassing a diverse botanical reserve.

Edible Shrubs contains plants that are familiar specimens growing in my garden, for example gooseberries, thyme and blackcurrants, Chilean Guava (*Ugni Molinae*), Ramanas Rose (*Rosa Rugosa*). Others have been on my 'must grow next year list' for some time such as the Siberian Pea-tree (*Caragana Boisii*) or the Japanese Quince (*Chaenomeles Speciosa*). Many, however, are completely new to me and the adventure will start as I plan what to plant and how to integrate some of them into my polyculture space. I love the idea that the humble gooseberry or blackcurrant, along with their other woody companions have the capacity to change the world!

The shrubs listed here include something for every type of growing space however large or small and suited to different climates and growing situations. Perennials also lend themselves to endless propagation and from a few stock plants many thousands can follow. By itself, this is a form of resistance and self-reliance that is beyond of the grasp of our current leaders and one that can be shared amongst people outside of any given economic system.

Our counterparts in the perennial plant world have the qualities of being resilient, adaptive, tenacious, nourishing, fruitful, diverse and medicinal. We need to look to them and this book for inspiration as to how we make change now with plants for the future.

Armed with my well-thumbed and grubby copy of PFAF's *Edible Perennials* in one hand and my shiny new copy of *Edible Shrubs* in the other, I'm ready to perennialise the planet.

Mandy Barber
Plant researcher, grower, founder of Incredible Vegetables Project, Dartmoor, Devon, UK

Introduction

Edible Shrubs is the fifth in a series of illustrated reference books from Plants For A Future (PFAF). This book provides information on over 70 selected shrubs, most of which produce delicious and nutritious fruit, but many also have edible leaves, seeds, flowers, stems or roots, or yield oil. Most of these plants also have medicinal properties and other uses such as for fibres or dyes. We have included several plants that may not be well known to growers, to encourage them to try out different food crops in new combinations and plot designs. Some of the plants described are also included in our earlier books but here we are providing more detailed information than before.

Shrubs are particularly important for their role in food forests or woodland gardens, where they occupy the highly productive layer between the canopy and the ground. To give you a wide choice, the shrubs we have selected vary in height from a few inches tall to as big as trees (if you let them). As perennial woody plants, shrubs help to draw down and sequester carbon from the atmosphere, a vital function in today's world. Growing food locally, for year-round yields, also reduces carbon dioxide emissions from transportation and refrigeration.

Details on each of the featured shrubs are taken from plant pages of the PFAF database. The database has a thirty year history: twenty years as the repository of experience and research findings by Ken Fern, a leading expert in alternative food crops for temperate climate zones, followed by ten years being further developed and refined by the PFAF charity. During the new phase of PFAF from 2008 onwards, the plant entries were checked and expanded with additional data items including hardiness settings, weed potential and conservation status. Most importantly, images of the plants have been added to the database to aid identification.

In this book, we include a wide range of plants that are suitable for temperate zones, but also additional plants that can be grown in warmer areas. Where possible we have chosen plants that have adapted to different conditions. It is very pleasing that the database has become recognised as a high quality source of information and that its usage has increased over time. We now have over 2 million accesses per year from users all over the world and from every climate zone.

It was in 2012 that we decided to publish the first of a series of illustrated reference books. Our intention was to offer selected information from our website and database in an attractive format, to expand our user base and hopefully produce some book sales revenue to supplement our income from donations. *Edible Shrubs* is the fifth in this series, and also the third of a set of books related to woodland garden design, following *Edible Trees* in 2013 and *Edible Perennials* in 2015.

Edible Trees and *Edible Perennials* featured 50 favourite plants each, and for *Edible Shrubs* a similar number of main plants was selected, and it was decided to add supporting plants from the same genus if appropriate. For example, we include four hazel species which are worth considering if you are planning a garden. Since they are very similar, only one has full details, to avoid repetition. Entries for the additional plants feature the differences (e.g. height or fruit/nut size) rather than similarities. Recent work to add 230 Carbon Farming plants (see below) led to the decision to introduce a number of other plants with edible qualities, especially if they were in the same genus as a plant already included. So *Edible Shrubs* includes details and images of 73 plants, with a Plant Species Matrix showing the main features of 400 additional plants.

Carbon Farming

The PFAF database now includes information on approximately 7,700 useful plants, including around 700 plants suited to tropical climate zones. Researching and adding the new tropical plants was a project for 2016-17, funded by our Annual Appeal and a grant from the Schöck Family Trust. Over that period it was discovered that there was a considerable overlap between the set of new plants we had identified and the 'Species Matrix' which is key to the important book on Carbon Farming by Eric Toensmeier, which was published in 2016.

PFAF has always focused on perennial crops and on providing information on ecologically sustainable horticulture. Some of these crops, as well as being suitable for gardens and small scale growers, can also be used in larger scale agriculture. In Toensmeier's book, the full title of which is *The Carbon Farming Solution: A Global Toolkit of Perennial Crops and Regenerative Agriculture Practices for Climate Change Mitigation and Food Security*, he identifies several hundred plants that can be a critical part of the solution to climate problems. In Edible Shrubs we have included a number of these potentially important plants, with brief details of their relevance to Carbon Farming.

Climate change is one of the most significant issues facing our planet. People all over the world are trying to find ways to slow the progression of, and ultimately reverse, damage to the environment. Changes in farming practices to make greater use of perennials will be a considerable step towards carbon sequestration and climate change mitigation. The idea is simple enough. Plants that are grown annually: harvested once before they die, take valuable resources from the Earth. A perennial is planted once and then lives for several years, lowering the impact on the environment. If the food we eat could be planted once but harvested several times during its life-cycle, the adverse effects on the environment would be significantly lowered.

Botanic Name	CommonName	Zone	ER	MR	OR	Shade	Water	M	Ft	Edible Part	Harvest	CF	Page
Abutilon megapotamicum	Trailing Abutilon	7 to 10	4	0	0	SN	M	2	6' 7"	Flowers	Sp to A		54
Acca sellowiana	Feijoa	8 to 11	4	0	2	N	DM	3	9' 10"	Flowers; Fruit	Sp to A		26
Aloysia triphylla	Lemon Verbena	7 to 10	4	3	3	SN	DM	3	9' 10"	Leaves	Sp to A (W)		34
Amelanchier alnifolia	Saskatoon	4 to 6	5	2	3	SN	M	4	13' 1"	Fruit	Su		46
Amelanchier canadensis	Serviceberry	4 to 7	4	1	4	SN	M	6	19' 8"	Fruit	Su		47
Aronia melanocarpa	Black Chokeberry	3 to 8	3	1	2	SN	DM	2.5	8' 2"	Fruit	Su		12
Atriplex halimus	Saltbush	7 to 10	5	1	3	N	DM	2	6' 7"	Leaves; Manna; Seed	All		44
Atriplex semibaccata	Australian Saltbush	8 to 11	3	0	4	N	DM	0.5	1' 6"	Fruit; Leaves	All		45
Atriplex truncata	Wedgeleaf Saltbush	7 to 10	2	0	4	N	DM	1	3' 3"	Leaves; Seed	All	Y	45
Berberis aristata	Indian Barberry	5 to 9	4	3	3	SN	DM	3.5	11' 6"	Flowers; Fruit	SpSu		9
Cajanus cajan	Pigeon Pea	9 to 12	4	2	4	N	M	4	13' 1"	Seeds; Leaves; Shoots	Su to W	Y	39
Caragana arborescens	Siberian Peashrub	2 to 7	5	1	4	N	DM	6	19' 8"	Oil; Seed; Seedpod	Su to A	Y	37
Caragana boisii	Siberian Peatree	2 to9	4	0	4	N	DM	2	6' 7"	Oil; Seed; Seedpod	Su to A		38
Caragana brevispina	Pea Tree	4 to 9	4	1	3	N	DM	2.5	8' 2"	Leaves; Seed	Su to A		38
Caragana microphylla	Littleleaf Peashrub	5 to 9	2	0	4	SN	DM	1.5	4' 11"	Seed; Seedpod	Su to A	Y	37
Castanea pumila	Chinquapin	4 to 8	4	1	2	SN	DM	4	13' 1"	Seed	Su to A		18
Cephalotaxus harringtonia	Japanese Plum Yew	6 to 9	5	0	3	FS	M	5	16' 5"	Fruit; Oil; Seed	A		32
Chaenomeles speciosa	Flowering Quince	4 to 8	3	2	3	FSN	M	3	9' 10"	Fruit	A		40
Chrysobalanus icaco	Coco Plum	10 to 12	4	2	3	SN	DM	6	19' 8"	Fruit; Seeds	Sp to A	Y	19
Cnidoscolus aconitifolius	Tree Spinach	9 to 11	4	3	2	SN	M	5	16' 5"	Leaves;Shoot	All	Y	55
Cordeauxia edulis	Yeheb	10 to 12	3	0	4	N	DM	4	13' 1"	Leaves; Seed	Su	Y	57
Cornus mas	Cornelian Cherry	4 to 8	4	2	0	SN	M	5	16' 5"	Fruit; Oil	Su to A		20
Cornus sericea	Red Osier	3 to 7	5	2	4	SN	MWe	2.5	8' 2"	Fruit; Oil; Seed.	Su	Y	41
Corylus cornuta californica	California Hazel	5 to 9	5	2	0	FSN	DM	5	16' 5"	Fruit; Seed	A		29
Corylus avellana	Hazelnut	4 to 8	5	5	2	N	DMWe	6	19' 8"	Fruit; Oil	A	Y	30
Corylus heterophylla	Siberian Filbert	4 to 8	4	2	1	N	DM	7	22' 12"	Oil; Seed	A	Y	30
Corylus sieboldiana	Manchurian hazel	5 to 9	3	0	0	SN	M	5	16' 5"	Oil; Seed	A	Y	29
Elaeagnus angustifolia	Oleaster	2 to 7	4	2	4	N	DM	7	22' 12"	Fruit; Seed	A	Y	51
Elaeagnus multiflora	Goumi	5 to 9	5	2	3	SN	DM	3	9' 10"	Fruit; Seed	Su		50
Elaeagnus x ebbingei	Silverberry	5 to 9	5	2	4	FSN	DM	5	16' 5"	Fruit; Seed	SpSu		49
Elaeagnus rhamnoides	Sea Buckthorn	3 to 7	5	5	5	N	DMWe	6	19' 8"	Fruit; Oil	A to Sp	Y	46
Elaeagnus umbellata	Japanese Silverberry	3 to 7	4	2	4	N	DM	4.5		Fruit; Seeds	Su to A	Y	50
Fuchsia coccinea	Scarlet fuchsia	8 to 11	4	0	1	SN	M	3.5	11' 6"	Fruit	Su to A		27
Fuchsia splendens	Platanillo	8 to 11	4	0	0	FSN	M	2	6' 7"	Fruit	Su to A		27
Gaultheria hispidula	Creeping Snowberry	5 to 9	4	1	4	S	MWe	0.2	0' 8"	Fruit; Leaves	Su to A		21
Gaultheria humifusa	Alpine Wintergreen	6 to 9	4	0	3	SN	M	0.2	0' 8"	Fruit; Leaves	Sp to A		8

Zone = USDA Hardiness Zones. ER= Edible Rating. MR= Medicinal Rating. OR= Other Rating. M and Ft = size (metric or imperial).
Harvest: Sp= Spring, Su= Summer, A= Autumn, W= Winter. CF= Carbon farming

Scientific Name	Common Name		5	2	3	FS	DM						
Gaultheria shallon	Shallon	8 to 11	5	2	3	FS	DM	1.3	4' 3"	Fruit	Su		48
Gaylussacia baccata	Black Huckleberry	5 to 9	4	1	0	SN	DM	1	3' 3"	Fruit	Su		12
Hibiscus syriacus	Rose Of Sharon	5 to 9	4	2	2	SN	M	3	9' 10"	Flowers; Leaves; Oil; Root	Sp to A		41
Juniperus communis	Juniper	4 to 10	3	3	4	SN	DM	9	29' 6"	Fruit; Leaves; Seed	All		33
Lonicera angustifolia	Narrow-leafed honeysuckle	4 to 8	4	0	2	N	M	2.8	9' 2"	Fruit	Su		30
Lonicera villosa	Mountain fly honeysuckle	3 to 9	3	0	0	N	M	1.5	4' 11"	Fruit	Su		31
Lonicera caerulea	Sweetberry Honeysuckle	0 to 0	3	0	0	N	M	2	6' 7"	Fruit	Su		31
Lycium barbarum	Wolfberry Boxthorn	6 to 9	4	3	3	SN	M	2.5	8' 2"	Fruit; Leaves	Su to A		13
Lycium chinense	Chinese Boxthorn	5 to 9	4	3	3	N	M	2.5	8' 2"	Fruit; Leaves; Seed	Su to A		14
Morella cerifera	Wax Myrtle	7 to 11	3	3	3	SN	M	9	29' 6"	Fruit; Leaves	All	Y	56
Mahonia aquifolium	Oregon Grape	4 to 8	3	3	0	FSN	DM	2	6' 7"	Flowers; Fruit	AW		36
Myrteola nummularia	Cranberry Myrtle	7 to 10	4	0	4	N	DM	0.2	0' 8"	Fruit; Leaves	AW		21
Poncirus trifoliata	Bitter Orange	6 to 9	3	2	3	SN	M	3	9' 10"	Fruit; Leaves	A		11
Prinsepia utilis	Cherry Prinsepia	6 to 9	3	2	0	SN	M	3.5	11' 6"	Fruit; Oil	Su to W	Y	16
Prunus cerasifera	Cherry Plum	5 to 8	4	1	3	SN	M	9	29' 6"	Fruit; Seed	Su to A		15
Prunus laurocerasus	Cherry Laurel	6 to 8	4	3	5	FSN	M	6	19' 8"	Fruit; Seed	Su		15
Prunus sibirica	Siberian apricot	4 to 8	3	2	4	SN	M	3		Fruit; Oil; Seed	Su	Y	49
Prunus pumila	Dwarf American Cherry	3 to 8	4	1	2	N	DM	0.7	2' 4"	Fruit; Seed	Su		16
Rhus aromatica	Lemon Sumach	3 to 9	4	2	2	N	DM	1.3	4' 3"	Fruit; Oil	Sp to A		52
Rhus typhina	Stag's Horn Sumach	4 to 8	4	2	0	N	DM	6	19' 8"	Fruit; Oil	Su		53
Ribes aureum	Golden Currant	3 to 8	4	1	0	SN	DM	2.5	8' 2"	Flowers; Fruit	Su		22
Ribes nigrum	Blackcurrant	4 to 8	5	3	0	SN	M	1.8	5' 11"	Fruit; Leaves	Su		23
Ribes uva-crispa	Gooseberry	4 to 8	5	1	2	SN	M	1.3	4' 3"	Fruit; Leaves	SpSu		28
Rosa rugosa	Ramanas Rose	3 to 9	5	2	3	SN	M	2	6' 7"	Flowers; Fruit; Seed; Stem	Su to A		42
Rubus canadensis	American Dewberry	3 to 7	4	1	0	SN	M	2.5	8' 2"	Fruit	Su		8
Salvia officinalis	Sage	5 to 10	4	5	5	N	DM	0.7	2' 4"	Leaves; Flowers	All		43
Sambucus nigra	Elderberry	5 to 7	4	3	5	SN	M	6	19' 8"	Flowers; Fruit	Su to A	Y	24
Sambucus nigra spp canadensis	American Elder	3 to 9	4	3	5	SN	M	4	13' 1"	Flowers; Fruit; Leaves	Su to A	Y	25
Solanum muricatum	Pepino	8 to 11	4	0	0	N	M	1	3' 3"	Fruit	Su to W		38
Solanum quitoense	Naranjilla	10 to 12	4	0	0	SN	M	2.5	8' 2"	Fruit	All		35
Thymus vulgaris	Common Thyme	5 to 8	4	3	5	N	DM	0.3	0' 12"	Leaves; Flowers	All		53
Ugni molinae	Chilean guava	7 to 10	5	0	3	N	DM	2	6' 7"	Fruit; Leaves; Seed	A		17
Sambucus nigra	Elderberry	5 to 7	4	3	5	SN	M	6	19' 8"	Flowers; Fruit	Su to A	Y	24
Vaccinium corymbosum	High-Bush Blueberry	3 to 8	4	1	0	SN	M	2	6' 7"	Flowers; Fruit	Su		10
Vaccinium myrtillus	Bilberry	3 to 7	4	3	1	SN	M	0.3	0' 12"	Fruit; Leaves	A		10
Yucca baccata	Spanish Yucca	6 to 11	4	1	5	N	DM	0.9	2' 11"	Flowers; Fruit; Leaves; Seed; Stem	A	Y	57
Yucca filamentosa	Spoonleaf Yucca	4 to 10	3	1	4	SN	DM	1.3	4' 3"	Flowers; Fruit; Stem	A		58
Zanthoxylum piperitum	Japanese Pepper Tree	5 to 9	3	2	1	SN	M	2	6' 7"	Fruit; Leaves; Seed	W		32

Shade: F = full shade S = semi-shade N = no shade. **Water:** D = dry M = Moist We = wet Wa = water

Alpine Wintergreen

Gaultheria humifusa - (Graham.)Rydb.

Family: Ericaceae
Known Hazards: None known
Natural Habitats: Moist alpine and sub-alpine slopes.
Natural Range: Western N. America.
Hardiness Zones: USDA 6-9. UK 7.
Size: Shrub height 0.1m (0ft 4in). Some cultivars to 5ft
Growth: Medium
Soil: light (sandy) and medium (loamy) soils. It prefers moist soil.
Soil pH: acid and neutral soils and can grow in very acid soils.
Light: It can grow in semi-shade (light woodland) or no shade.
Edibility Rating: 4
Medicinal Rating: 0
Other Uses Rating: 3
Forest Garden: Sunny Edge; Dappled Shade; Ground Cover.

American Dewberry

Rubus canadensis - L.

Other names: Smooth blackberry, Thornless Blackberry
Family: Rosaceae
Known Hazards: None known
Natural Habitats: Thickets, woods and clearings.
Natural Range: North-eastern N. America - Newfoundland to Michigan and North Carolina.
Hardiness Zones: USDA 3-7. UK 3.
Size: Shrub growing to 2.5m (8ft)
Growth: Medium
Soil: light (sandy), medium (loamy) and heavy (clay) soils and prefers well-drained moist soil.
Soil pH: acid, neutral and basic (alkaline) soils.
Light: It can grow in semi-shade or no shade.
Edibility Rating: 4
Medicinal Rating: 1
Other Uses Rating: 1
Forest Garden: Sunny Edge; Dappled Shade.

Alpine Wintergreen

Gaultheria humifusa - (Graham.)Rydb.

—Harvest —   —Edible Part —
Small   6-9

Wintergreens are evergreen shrubs requiring a lime-free soil and some shade. They vary in height from a few inches to five feet, all of them having edible fruits. The Alpine Wintergreen grows to 0.1m (4in). The fruit is highly aromatic with a flavour that is somehow reminiscent of a hospital waiting room. Some people love them, others are a bit less sure. The leaves can be used to make a refreshing tea, and oil distilled from the plant (oil of wintergreen) is often used as a liniment in the treatment of muscular aches and pains.

Alpine wintergreen is a good ground cover plant for positions in the sun or light shade, with similar edible properties to Gaultheria hispidula, mentioned later. In addition, a black dye has been made from the plant. The fruit is aromatic and delicious with a flavour of wintergreen. It is used in preserves and as a wayside nibble. The young tender leaves are especially suited for use as greens. They have a delicate flavour of wintergreen.

Alpine wintergreen prefers a moist but not boggy humus-rich soil in sun or semi-shade. It grows well in a rock garden. It is closely allied to G. ovatifolia.

American Dewberry

Rubus canadensis - L.

—Harvest —   —Edible Part —
Large   3-7

The Rubus genus of deciduous and evergreen shrubs includes raspberries and blackberries and several ornamental species with edible fruits. American dewberry is a vigorous 'thornless' blackberry with an abundance of fruit after the second season. The fruit ripens in mid to late summer. The fruit is eaten raw or cooked in pies, jams etc. It is sweet, juicy and richly flavoured, and preferred to most other species of blackberries. The fruit can be pressed into cakes and then dried for later use. The fruit can be up to 25mm (1in) long.

The stems, fruit and root have been used in the treatment of dysentery. A purple to dull blue dye is obtained from the fruit.

American dewberry is easily grown in a good well-drained loamy soil in sun or semi-shade. It is a blackberry with biennial stems. It produces many new stems each year from the perennial rootstock. New stems fruit in their second year and then die. The stems are free from prickles. The plant produces apomictic flowers which produce fruit and viable seed without fertilization, each seedling being a genetic copy of the parent. Plants in this genus are notably susceptible to honey fungus.

Propagate by seed, cuttings, or layering. Seed requires stratification and is best sown in early autumn. Stored seed requires one-month stratification at about 3°C and is best sown as early as possible in the year. Cuttings of half-ripe wood are taken in summer. Tip layering is carried out in summer for planting out in the autumn. Divide in early spring or just before leaf-fall in the autumn.

Rubus canadensis

Barberry *Berberis species*

The genus comprises approximately 500 species of deciduous, evergreen shrubs found in the temperate and sub-tropical regions of Asia, Europe and America. The genus includes some extremely ornamental evergreen and deciduous shrubs, which tend to tolerate most soils and locations. None of them has poisonous fruits though many are unpalatable. B. vulgaris was once quite commonly grown in the fruit garden but has fallen out of favour. Because it is the alternate host of black stem rust on wheat, farmers have eradicated it from hedgerows and woodlands. Other species to consider are B. aggregata, B. angulosa, B. aristata, B. asiatica, B. buxifolia, B. darwinii and B. lycium. The fruits are acid but can be eaten raw (best after a frost) or used to make conserves, jams etc. They can also be dried and used as a substitute for raisins. Some species can be used to make very ornamental informal hedges, B. darwinii being especially good.

Indian Barberry

Berberis aristata -DC.

—Harvest —   —Edible Part —

Large   5-9

Indian Barberry is an erect spiny shrub in the genus Berberis with edible fruit and flowers and useful as a medicinal plant. The fruit is eaten raw or cooked and has a sweet taste with a blend of acid, though there is a slight bitterness caused by the seeds. Children like the fruit very much. It is dried and used like raisins in India. The fruit contains about 2.3% protein, 12% sugars, 2% ash, 0.6% tannin, 0.4% pectin. There is 4.6mg vitamin C per 100ml of juice. The fruit is available in early spring into summer and is about 7mm to 10mm long. They can remain on the shrub after ripening for quite a long period. Plants in the wild yield about 650g of fruit in four pickings. Flower buds are added to sauces.

In India, Indian Barberry is used in traditional herbal medicine. Its stem, roots and fruits are used in Ayurveda. Uses including an alterative, antibacterial, antiperiodic, bitter, deobstruent, diaphoretic, laxative, ophthalmic and tonic. The dried stem, root bark and wood are alterative, antiperiodic, deobstruent, diaphoretic, laxative, ophthalmic and tonic (bitter). Berberine, universally present in rhizomes of Berberis species, has marked antibacterial effects.

A yellow dye is obtained from the root and the stem. An important source of dyestuff and tannin, it is perhaps one of the best tannin dyes available in India. The wood is used as a fuel. The spiny branches are used for making fencing around fields.

Indian Barberry is very hardy. It prefers a warm moist loamy soil and light shade, but it is not fussy. It succeeds in thin, dry and shallow soils, and grows well in heavy clay soils. It can be pruned back quite severely and re-sprouts well from the base. The fruits are sold in local markets in India.

Propagate by seed or cuttings. Seed is sown as soon as it is ripe; it should germinate in late winter or early spring. Seed from over-ripe fruit will take longer to grow. Stored seed may require cold stratification and should be sown as early in the year as possible. Propagation by cutting is very difficult and seldom takes. Half-ripe wood is taken in summer. Take cuttings of mature wood of the current season's growth, preferably with a heel, in early winter.

Indian Barberry

Berberis aristata -DC.
Other names: Chitra or Tree Turmeric
Family: Berberidaceae
Known Hazards: None known
Natural Habitats: Shrubberies to 3500m. Open hillsides at elevations of 1800 - 3000m.
Natural Range: E. Asia - Himalayas in Nepal.
Hardiness Zones: USDA 5-9. UK 6.
Size: Shrub growing to 3.5m (11ft)
Growth: Medium
Soil: light (sandy), medium (loamy) and heavy (clay) soils and can grow in heavy clay and nutritionally poor soils. It prefers dry or moist soil.
Soil pH: Acid, neutral and basic (alkaline) soils.
Light: It can grow in semi-shade (light woodland) or no shade.
Edibility Rating: 4
Medicinal Rating: 3
Other Uses Rating: 3
Forest Garden: Dappled Shade; Shady Edge.

(0.4in) in diameter with one large seed. The fruit has a rich and pleasantly acid taste when fully ripe, though it is sometimes slightly bitter. The fruit is eaten straight from the bush, used in preserves or dried for later use. Fruit and seed can be eaten raw or cooked. Do not eat the seed if it is too bitter.

Although no specific mention of toxicity has been seen for this species, all members of the genus contain amygdalin and prunasin, substances which break down in water to form hydrocyanic acid (cyanide or prussic acid). In small amounts, this exceedingly poisonous compound stimulates respiration, improves digestion and gives a sense of well-being.

A green dye can be obtained from the leaves, and a dark grey to green colour can be obtained from the fruit. Dwarf American cherry is used as a rootstock for the sour cherry.

Dwarf American cherry requires a well-drained moisture retentive soil and thrives in a loamy soil, doing well on limestone. It prefers some chalk in the soil but apt to become chlorotic if too much is present. It requires a sunny position. Once established it is very drought resistant. It is hardy to about -35°C when fully dormant, though the young growth in spring is relatively tender. It is susceptible to mildew in low areas. It thrives in areas with a short growing season. The fruits are highly resistant to all fruit worms. It can produce fruit in 3 years from seed. Most members of this genus are shallow-rooted and will produce suckers if the roots are damaged.

Propagate by seed, cuttings and layering. The seed requires 2–3 months of cold stratification and is best sown in a cold frame as soon as it is ripe. Sow stored seed as early in the year as possible. The seed can be somewhat slow, sometimes taking 18 months to germinate. Cuttings of half-ripe wood with a heel, are taken mid-summer. Softwood cuttings from actively growing plants are made in spring to early summer. Layering is possible in spring.

Chilean Guava

Ugni molinae - Turcz.

—Harvest —   —Edible Part —

Medium   Z 7-10

Ugni molinae, commonly known as Chilean guava, strawberry myrtle, Ugniberry, or New Zealand cranberry, is an evergreen shrub growing to 2m (6ft). It is an excellent ornamental plant with a beautiful strawberry aroma. Chilean guava is often planted as a low growing hedge or a container specimen. It was a favourite fruit of Queen Victoria, introduced to the UK in 1844.

The fruit has a delicious flavour, it is very aromatic and tastes of wild strawberries. The fruit is about 15mm in diameter, harvested in autumn, and is freely borne even on small plants. The fruit is used to make jam, Kuchen cake and the dessert murta con membrillo. The leaves are a tea substitute. The roasted seeds are a coffee substitute. In Chile it is used to make the traditional liqueur Murtado.

Chilean guava can be grown as a small hedge and tolerates trimming. It succeeds in any reasonably good soil including dry ones. It prefers a moderately fertile well-drained loam in a sunny position and is fairly tolerant of maritime exposure. Once established it is drought resistant. It is a very ornamental plant. It is only hardy in milder temperate areas, tolerating temperatures down to about

Dwarf American Cherry

Prunus pumila - L.
Other names: Western or Eastern Sandcherry,
Family: Rosaceae
Known Hazards: See Prunus sibirica
Natural Habitats: Dunes and sand, or on calcareous rocky shores.
Natural Range: Eastern N. America
Hardiness Zones: USDA 3 - 8. UK 2.
Size: Shrub growing to 0.6m (2ft)
Growth: Medium
Soil: light (sandy), medium (loamy) and heavy (clay) soils and prefers well-drained, dry to moist soil. It can tolerate drought and strong winds.
Soil pH: Acid, neutral and basic (alkaline) soils.
Light: It cannot grow in the shade.
Edibility Rating: 4
Medicinal Rating: 1
Other Uses Rating: 2
Forest Garden: Sunny Edge; Dappled Shade.

Chilean Guava

Ugni molinae - Turcz.
Other names: Uñi
Family: Myrtaceae
Known Hazards: None known
Natural Habitats: Woodland edges and scrub.
Natural Range: S. America - Chile.
Hardiness Zones: USDA 7-10. UK 8.
Size: Shrub growing to 2m (6ft)
Growth: Medium
Soil: light (sandy), medium (loamy) and heavy (clay) soils and prefers well-drained, dry or moist soil and can tolerate drought.
Soil pH: Acid, neutral and basic (alkaline) soils.
Light: It cannot grow in the shade.
The plant can tolerate strong winds but not maritime exposure.
Edibility Rating: 5
Other Uses Rating: 3
Forest Garden: Sunny Edge; Hedge.

-10°C when fully dormant. The young growth in spring can be damaged by late frosts. Chilean guava is a much underused plant that merits cultivation on a commercial scale for its fruit. It flowers and fruits well even when the plants are young. Plants in this genus are notably resistant to honey fungus.

Propagation is by seed, cuttings and layering. Pre-soak the seed for 24 hours in warm water and then sow it in late winter in a greenhouse in colder areas. Cuttings of half-ripe wood and are taken 7–10cm (4in) with a heel in mid-summer in a coldframe. Pot up in the autumn and plant out in late spring. Cuttings of mature wood of the current season's growth are taken 7–12cm (4in) with a heel in early winter in a shaded and frost free position. Plant out in late spring or early autumn. Cuttings are very successful. Layering is also possible.

Chinquapin

Castanea pumila -(L.)Mill
Other names: Ozark chinkapin
Family: Fagaceae
Known Hazards: None known
Natural Habitats: Dry sandy ridges and rich hillsides where it forms thickets, also in woods and on the borders of swamps.
Natural Range: Eastern N. America - New Jersey and Pennsylvania to Florida, Missouri and Texas.
Hardiness Zones: USDA 4-8. UK 5.
Size: Shrub growing to 4m (13ft)
Growth: Slow
Soil: Light (sandy), medium (loamy) and heavy (clay) soils. Prefers well-drained dry or moist soil. Grows in nutritionally poor soil. Tolerates drought.
Soil pH: Acid and neutral soils and can grow in very acid soils.
Light: It cannot grow in the shade.
Edibility Rating: 4
Medicinal Rating: 1
Other Uses Rating: 2
Forest Garden: Secondary layer; Sunny Edge; Dappled Shade.

Chinquapin

Castanea pumila -(L.)Mill

—Harvest —   —Edible Part —

🞕 💧 ◐ 📶 *Large* **Z** *4-8*

Chinquapin is a spreading shrub or small tree, closely related to the American chestnut, Castanea dentata. It is commonly known as the Allegheny chinquapin, American chinquapin or dwarf chestnut. It has smaller leaves and fruit than other chestnuts. Nuts are harvested in late summer into autumn.

The sweet, nutty flavoured seeds are very acceptable raw with a superior flavour to sweet chestnuts (C. sativa). When baked the seeds become even more delicious and develop a floury texture, making an excellent potato or cereal substitute. The seed is quite small, about 2cm (1in) thick, which is about half the size of C. dentata. It is sold in local markets in America. The seed husks only contain one seed, rarely two. The seed contains 45% starch and 2.5% protein.

Chinquapin leaves contain tannin and are antiperiodic, astringent and tonic. An infusion of the leaves has been used as an external wash for the feverish condition common to colds.

The bark, leaves, wood and seed husks all contain useful tannin. The wood is coarse-grained, hard, light, durable, and easy to split. It is too small for commercial use, and occasionally used for fence posts, fuel etc. It weighs 37lb per cubic foot.

Chinquapin prefers a good, well-drained, slightly acid loam soil and can succeed in dry soils. Once established, it is very tolerant of drought and of highly acid, infertile, dry sands. It is averse to calcareous soils but succeeds on harder limestones. This species is an excellent soil-enriching understorey in pine forests, growing and fruiting well so long as the canopy of pines is relatively light. Although it is very winter-hardy, this species only really thrives in areas with hot summers. The young growth in spring, even on mature plants, is frost-tender and so it is best to grow the plant in a position sheltered from the early morning sun. It can spread widely using underground suckers. Flowers are produced on the wood of the current year's growth. It is fairly self-sterile. It hybridizes freely with other members of the genus. Fruits are produced in 2 to 3 years from seed. Chinquapin does not like coastal salt conditions, but the sub-species C. pumila ashei is a coastal form, found from Virginia to Texas. Plants in this genus are notably resistant to honey fungus.

Propagation is by seed or the division of suckers. The seed is sown as soon as it is ripe, and must be protected from mice and squirrels. The seed has a short viability and must not be allowed to become dry. It can be stored for a few months in a cool place, such as the salad compartment of a fridge if it is kept moist, but must be regularly checked for signs of germination. Suckers can be divided in winter and planted straight out into their permanent positions.

Coco Plum

Chrysobalanus icaco -L

—Harvest —   —Edible Part —

Large   10-12

Coco plum is a widely cultivated food plant commonly found near sea beaches and inland. It is a small evergreen tree or a shrub that grows up to 6m tall.

The fruit of the Coco plum is eaten raw or cooked and has a fairly sweet, white, spongy flesh. They are stewed in sugar, dried like prunes or made into jams and jellies. The purple or red-skinned ovoid fruit is 2–5cm (2in) long and is considered to have a superior flavour to the white forms. The seed is eaten raw or cooked and has a delicious flavour. When cooked they are usually roasted. To preserve the fruit, pierce them right through the centre, including the seed. This allows the juice of the fruit to penetrate the seed and, after separation from the shell, the nut-like kernel is eaten. Edible oil is extracted from the seed.

Coco plum is a useful ornamental shrub for dry and salty conditions. It can be grown in the garden for screening, in a planter and for topiary. It can be grown as a hedge in an agroforestry system. It can form large, rambling, impenetrable thickets suitable for stabilising dunes.

The seeds are so rich in oil that they can be strung on sticks and burnt like candles. The bark is rich in tannins. A black dye is obtained from the fruit and the leaves.

Medicinally, it is used internally against dysentery, dyspepsia and diarrhoea and externally against various skin conditions.

Coco plum can grow in very acid and saline soils. It likes semi-shade (light woodland) or full sun. The fruits are harvested in spring, summer and autumn, with larger crops in early spring and autumn.

Coco plum is an excellent Carbon Farming Solution plant for a staple protein-oil crop. For agroforestry it can be used as a living fence.

Coco Plum

Chrysobalanus icaco -L
Other names: Paradise Plum
Family: Chrysobalanaceae
Hardiness Zones: USDA 10-12. UK 10
Known Hazards: None known
Natural Habitats: Forests near the shore line. Coastal shoreline and sandy thickets. Usually found where the soil is moist or flooded.
Range: S. America from Brazil, to the Caribbean, Mexico and southern Florida. West tropical Africa - coastal areas from Senegal to Angola.
Size: Evergreen shrub growing to 6m (19ft)
Growth: Slow
Soil: Light (sandy), medium (loamy) and heavy (clay) soils and prefers well-drained soil.
Soil pH: Acid, neutral and basic (alkaline) soils and can grow in very acid and saline soils. It prefers moist soil and can tolerate drought. The plant can tolerate strong winds but not maritime exposure.
Light: It can grow in semi-shade (light woodland) or no shade.
Edibility Rating: 4
Medicinal Rating: 2
Other Uses: 3
Weed Potential: Yes
It is noted for attracting wildlife.
Carbon Farming: A staple protein-oil crop. A regional crop. Agroforestry Services: Living fence. Management: Standard

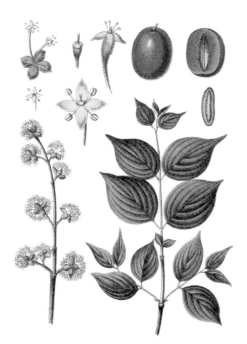

Cornelian Cherry

Cornus mas -L
Other names: Cornelian Cherry Dogwood
Family: Cornaceae
Known Hazards: None known
Natural Habitats: Woodlands, especially in calcareous soils.
Natural Range: Europe. Naturalized in Britain.
Hardiness Zones: USDA 4-8. UK 5.
Size: Shrub growing to 5m (16ft)
Growth: Medium
Soil: Light (sandy), medium (loamy) and heavy (clay) soils and can grow in heavy clay soil. It prefers moist soil.
The plant can tolerate strong winds but not maritime exposure.
Soil pH: Acid, neutral and basic (alkaline) soils and can grow in very alkaline soils.
Light: It can grow in semi-shade (light woodland) or no shade.
Edibility Rating: 4
Medicinal Rating: 2
Other Uses Rating: 3
Forest Garden: Sunny Edge; Dappled Shade; Hedge.

Cornelian Cherry

Cornus mas -L

—Harvest —   —Edible Part —

Large   4-8

Cornelian cherry is a medium to a large deciduous shrub or small tree often used as an ornamental for its late winter flowers that open even before Forsythia. The small yellow flowers growing in dense plumes are loved by bees and are excellent for attracting pollinators in early spring.

The fruit, ready from summer to autumn, is eaten raw, dried or used in preserves. It is juicy, with a lovely acid flavour. The fully ripe fruit has a somewhat plum-like taste and texture and is very lovely, but the unripe fruit is slightly astringent. It is low in pectin and so needs to be used with other fruit when making jam. At one time the fruit was kept in brine and used like olives. The fruit is a reasonable size, up to 15mm (0.6in) long, with a single large seed. A small amount of edible oil can be extracted from the seeds. Seeds are roasted, ground into a powder and used as a coffee substitute.

Cornelian cherry has some medical uses. The bark and the fruit are astringent, febrifuge and nutritive. The astringent fruit is a good treatment for bowel complaints and fevers, while it is also used in the treatment of cholera. The flowers are used in the treatment of diarrhoea.

Oil is obtained from the seed, a dye from the bark, and the leaves are a good source of tannin. The wood is tough; woodturners value it highly. The wood is heavier than water and does not float. It is used for tools, machine parts, etc. Landscape uses include borders, hedges, screens, a specimen plant and in woodland / forest gardens.

Cornelian cherry is an easily grown plant, which succeeds in any soil of good or moderate fertility, ranging from acid to shallow chalk. It will also grow well in heavy clay soils. It prefers moist soil and a sunny position but will succeed in light shade. It is relatively wind resistant. It grows and crops well in pots. It is a very hardy plant, tolerating temperatures down to about -25°C. At one time the cornelian cherry was frequently cultivated for its edible fruit, though it has fallen into virtual disuse as a fruit crop in most areas. It is still being cultivated in parts of Central Europe and there are some named varieties. The variety 'Macrocarpa' has larger fruits than the type. 'Nana' is a dwarf form, derived from a yellow-fruited clone. 'Variegata' has been seen on many occasions with large crops of fruit, even in years when the type species has not fruited well. 'Jolico' has well-flavoured fruits three times larger than the species. There are also some cultivars with yellow, white and purplish fruit. Seedlings can take up to 20 years to come into fruit. Plants produced from cuttings come into fruit when much younger, though they do not live as long as the seedlings. Cornelian cherry is a very ornamental plant which flowers quite early in the year and is a valuable early food for bees. Plants in this genus are notably resistant to honey fungus and are pest tolerant.

Propagation is by seed, cuttings and layering. The seed is best sown as soon as it is ripe. The seed must be separated from the fruit flesh since this contains germination inhibitors. Stored seed should be cold stratified for 3–4 months and sown as early as possible in the year. Germination, especially of stored seed, can be very slow, taking 18 months or more. Cuttings are easy and very successful. Cuttings of half-ripe side shoots are taken in mid-summer. Cuttings of mature wood of the current year's growth are taken, with a heel if possible, in autumn. Layering of new growth is done in early summer and takes nine months.

Cranberry Myrtle

Myrteola nummularia - (Poir.)O.Berg.

—Harvest —   —Edible Part —

Small Z 7-10

Cranberry myrtle is a hardy, evergreen, prostrate shrub making an excellent groundcover plant. The fruit has a soft juicy flesh and a delicious sweet, slightly aromatic flavour. The fruit is produced in late autumn and early winter and is up to 1cm in diameter. It is a valuable fruit at this time of the year. The leaves are a tea substitute.

Cranberry myrtle is suitable for ground cover when spaced about 45cm (1.5ft) apart each way. It forms a carpet of low branches that root as they spread. It is rather slow to become established and will need weeding for its first few years after planting.

Cranberry myrtle succeeds in any reasonably good soil including dry soils. It prefers a moderately fertile well-drained loam in a sunny position and will tolerate maritime exposure. It is not very hardy when grown outdoors in cooler temperate areas. It is a good carpeting plant for moist stones etc. in a rockery. Plants in this genus are notably resistant to honey fungus.

Propagate by seed, cuttings or layering. Pre-soak the seed for 24 hours in warm water and then sow it in late winter. Cuttings are very successful. Cuttings of half-ripe wood are taken, 7–10cm (4in) with a heel, in mid-summer. Cuttings of mature wood of the current season's growth are taken, 7–12cm (4in) with a heel, in early winter in a shaded location. Plant out in late spring or early autumn. Layering is possible.

Cranberry Myrtle has been awarded the RHS Award of Merit.

Cranberry Myrtle

Myrteola nummularia - (Poir.)O.Berg.
Family: Myrtaceae
Known Hazards: None known
Natural Habitats: Raised parts of bogs, especially with sphagnum.
Natural Range: S. America - S. Chile, Falklands.
Hardiness Zones: USDA 7-10. UK 8.
Size: Shrub growing to 0.1m (0ft 4in)
Growth: Slow
Soil: light (sandy), medium (loamy) and heavy (clay) soils and prefers well-drained, dry to moist soil.
The plant can tolerate maritime exposure.
Soil pH: acid, neutral and basic (alkaline) soils.
Light: It cannot grow in the shade.
Edibility Rating: 4
Medicinal Rating: 0
Other Uses Rating: 3
Forest Garden: Ground Cover; Cultivated Beds.

Creeping Snowberry

Gaultheria hispidula - (L.)Muhl. ex Bigelow.

—Harvest —   —Edible Part —

Small Z 5-9

Creeping snowberry is an evergreen fast-growing, prostrate shrub useful as a ground cover plant for shady positions. The fruit is pleasantly acid and refreshing, with a delicate flavour of wintergreen. It has a pleasant sub-acid taste, similar to G. shallon. The fruit, about 6mm (0.2in) in diameter, is made into delicious preserves. Both the fruit and the leaves can be eaten raw or cooked. The leaves are used to make a tea. A mild flavour of wintergreen is said to be superior to china tea. An infusion of the leaves are used as a tonic for someone who has overeaten.

Creeping snowberry prefers a moist but not boggy humus-rich soil in shade or semi-shade. A peat and moisture-loving species, it requires a lime-free soil. The fruit is sold in local markets. The plant can make a good nesting place for mice,

Creeping Snowberry

Gaultheria hispidula - (L.)Muhl. ex Bigelow.
Family: Ericaceae
Known Hazards: None known
Natural Habitats: Coniferous forests and mountains in the alpine and sub-alpine zones. Cold wet woods and bogs.
Natural Range: Northern N. America.
Hardiness Zones: USDA 5-9. UK 6.
Size: Shrub growing to 0.1m (0ft 4in)
Growth: Fast
Soil: light (sandy) and medium (loamy) soils. It prefers moist or wet soil.
Soil pH: acid and neutral soils and can grow in very acid soils.
Light: It can grow in semi-shade (light woodland).
Edibility Rating: 4
Medicinal Rating: 1
Other Uses Rating: 4
Forest Garden: Sunny Edge; Dappled Shade; Shady Edge; Ground Cover; Bog Garden.

Gaultheria hispidula

which eat the bark of the stems in winter causing die-back. Plants in this genus are notably resistant to honey fungus.

The seed requires a period of cold stratification. Pre-chill for 4–10 weeks and then surface sow in a lime-free compost. The seed usually germinates well, within one to two months at 20°C, but the seedlings are liable to damp off. Cuttings of half-ripe wood 3–6cm (2in) long, are taken in summer placed in a shady position. They form roots in late summer or spring. Division is possible in spring just before new growth begins. Larger clumps can be replanted direct into their permanent positions. Layering is also possible.

Golden Currant

Ribes aureum - Pursh.

— Harvest —   — Edible Part —

Golden currant is a member of the subgenus Ribes which contains other currants, such as the blackcurrant and redcurrant (Ribes nigrum and rubrum). It is a small to medium-sized deciduous shrub growing to 2–3m (6–10ft) which will tolerate dry areas in the garden. Golden currant is one of the first fruits to flower in early spring and is a good bee plant.

The berries are fairly large (about 5mm, 0.2in in diameter) and flavourful, can be eaten raw or cooked and make an acceptable dessert fruit. The fruit is among the tastiest of the American native currants. It ripens in mid-summer and is used in jellies, sauces and pies and dried for winter use. The flowers are eaten raw and have a very sweet flavour.

Medicinally the dried and pulverized inner bark has been sprinkled on sores. A decoction of the inner bark is used in the treatment of leg swellings.

Golden currant is easily grown in a moisture retentive but well-drained loamy soil. It succeeds in full sun but is also quite tolerant of shade, though not fruiting so well in such a position. It grows well on exposed dry sites and is very tolerant of being transplanted. It can spread using underground rhizomes, especially in moist conditions. It is hardy to about -20°C. The fruit can be red, black, yellow, golden or reddish-brown. Golden currant is a very ornamental plant, closely allied to R. odoratum. It can harbour a stage of white pine blister rust, so should not be grown in the vicinity of pine trees.

Propagate by seed and cuttings. Seed is best sown as soon as it is ripe in the autumn. Stored seed requires three months cold stratification at -2 to +2°C and should be sown as early in the year as possible. Under normal storage conditions, the seed can remain viable for 17 years or more. Cuttings of half-ripe wood, 10–15cm with a heel, are taken in summer. Cuttings of mature wood of the current year's growth, preferably with a heel of the previous year's growth, are taken in early winter.

Golden Currant

Ribes aureum - Pursh.
Family: Grossulariaceae
Known Hazards: None known
Natural Habitats: By streams, in ravines and on mountain slopes. Rocky slopes and sandy bluffs.
Natural Range: Western N. America - Saskatchewan to Washington, south to California. Naturalized in C. Europe.
Hardiness Zones: USDA 3 - 8. UK 2.
Size: Shrub growing to 2.4m (7ft 10in)
Growth: Fast
Soil: light (sandy), medium (loamy) and heavy (clay) soils and prefers well-drained, dry or moist soil.
Soil pH: acid, neutral and basic (alkaline) soils.
Light: It can grow in semi-shade or no shade. The plant can tolerate strong winds but not maritime exposure.
Edibility Rating : 4
Medicinal Rating: 1
Other Uses Rating: 0
Forest Garden: Sunny Edge; Dappled Shade.

Blackcurrant

Ribes nigrum - L.

—Harvest—   −Edible Part−

Medium   **Z** *4-8*

Blackcurrant is widely cultivated both commercially and domestically, being a fantastic addition to the garden. The fruit has an excellent aromatic flavour. It is known as the 'King of Berries' due to its potent antioxidant activity and powerful nutritional profile. The fully ripe fruit is very acceptable raw, though it is more often cooked and used to make pies, jams etc. It is very rich in vitamin C. The fruit is about 10mm in diameter, with selected cultivars having larger fruits. Use fresh leaves in soups and dried leaves as a tea substitute. Dried leaves are added to blended herb teas.

Blackcurrant has been used medicinally for uses including antidiarrhoeal, antirheumatic, diaphoretic, diuretic and as a febrifuge. Blackcurrant fruit is an excellent source of minerals and vitamins, especially vitamin C. It has diuretic and diaphoretic actions, helps to increase bodily resistance to infections and is a valuable remedy for treating colds and flu. The juice, especially when fresh or vacuum-sealed, helps to stem diarrhoea and calms indigestion. The leaves are cleansing, diaphoretic and diuretic.

The oil from the seed is added to skin preparations and cosmetics. It is often combined with vitamin E to prevent oxidation. A yellow dye is obtained from the leaves and a blue or violet colour from the fruit. The leaves are used for vegetable preservation.

Blackcurrant is easily grown in a moisture retentive but well-drained loamy soil of at least moderate quality. It prefers a deep sandy loam but can succeed on most soil types if plenty of organic matter is added. It dislikes very heavy clay, chalky soils and thin, dry soils. It requires plenty of nitrogen if it is to do well. It prefers a pH in the range 6.7 to 7 and is intolerant of acid soils. It is quite tolerant of shade but does not fruit so well in such a position or on windy sites. The plant is hardy to about -20°C, although its flowers are damaged at -1°C. Most fruit is produced on one-year-old wood. Pruning usually consists of removing about a third of all the stems from just above ground level in the autumn. The oldest stems with least new growth are removed since these will be the poorest fruiters. The plant is able to make new growth from the base of the removed stems and, if the plants are well fed, this growth is very vigorous and will fruit heavily the following year. The flowers can self-fertilize, but many cultivars fruit better with insect pollination. The plant can harbour a stage of 'white pine blister rust', so it should not be grown in the vicinity of pine trees.

Propagate by seed or cuttings. Seed is sown as soon as it is ripe in the autumn. Stored seed requires three months of cold stratification at between 0 and 5°C and should be sown as early in the year as possible. Cuttings of half-ripe wood are taken 10–15cm with a heel, in summer. Cuttings of mature wood of the current year's growth, preferably with a heel of the previous year's growth, can be taken in winter.

Blackcurrant

Ribes nigrum - L.
Family: Grossulariaceae
Known Hazards: None known
Natural Habitats: Hedges and woodlands, often by streams.
Natural Range: Europe, including Britain, from Scandinavia south and east to France, Bulgaria, N. and C. Asia.
Hardiness Zones: USDA 4-8. UK 5.
Size: Shrub growing to 1.8m (6ft)
Growth: Fast
Soil: Suitable for: light (sandy), medium (loamy) and heavy (clay) soils and prefers well-drained moist soil.
Soil pH: acid, neutral and basic (alkaline) soils.
Light: It can grow in semi-shade (light woodland) or no shade.
Edibility Rating: 5
Medicinal Rating: 3
Other Uses Rating: 2
Forest Garden: Sunny Edge; Dappled Shade; North Wall. East Wall.

Elderberry

Sambucus nigra - L

Other names: European Elder, American black elderberry, Blue elderberry

Family: Caprifoliaceae

Known Hazards: The leaves and stems are poisonous. The fruit of many species (although no records have been seen for this species) can cause stomach upsets to some people. Any toxin the fruit might contain is liable to be of very low toxicity and is destroyed when the fruit is cooked.

Natural Habitats: Hedgerows, scrub, woods, roadsides, waste places etc, especially on disturbed base-rich and nitrogen rich soils.

Natural Range: Europe, including Britain, from Scandinavia south and east to N. Africa and W. Asia.

Hardiness Zones: USDA 5-7. UK 5.

Size: Shrub growing to 6m (19ft)

Growth: Fast

Soil: light (sandy), medium (loamy) and heavy (clay) soils and can grow in heavy clay soil. It prefers moist soil. Can tolerate maritime exposure.
It can tolerate atmospheric pollution.

Soil pH: acid, neutral and basic (alkaline) soils and can grow in very alkaline soils.

Light: It can grow in semi-shade or no shade.

Edibility Rating: 4

Medicinal Rating: 3

Other Uses Rating: 5

Forest Garden: Sunny or Shady Edge; Dappled Shade; Hedge.

Carbon Farming: Industrial Crop: Dye; Medicinal. Management: Standard. Minor Global Crop.

Elderberry

Sambucus nigra - L

—Harvest —   —Edible Part —

Large   5-7

Elderberry is native to most of Europe and North America. It has excellent edible, medicinal and other uses. The flavour of the raw fruit is not acceptable to all tastes, though when cooked it makes delicious jams, preserves, pies etc. It can be used fresh or dried, the dried fruit being less bitter. The fruit is used to add flavour and colour to preserves, jams, pies, sauces, chutneys etc., and is used to make wine. The fruit is about 8mm in diameter and is borne in large clusters in late summer to early autumn. Flowers can be eaten raw, cooked or dried for later use. The flowers are crisp and somewhat juicy. They have an aromatic smell and flavour and are delicious raw as a refreshing snack on a summers day, though one must look out for insects. The flowers are used to add a muscatel flavour to stewed fruits, jellies and jams (especially gooseberry jam). They are often used to make a sparkling wine. Sweet tea is made from the dried flowers. The leaves are used to impart a green colouring to oils and fats.

Elderberry has a very long history of household use as a medicinal herb and is also much used by herbalists. The plant has been called 'the medicine chest of country people'. The flowers are the main part used in modern herbalism, though all parts of the plant have been used at times. The German Commission E Monographs, a therapeutic guide to herbal medicine, approves Elderberry for cough and bronchitis, fevers and colds.

Elderberry is a valuable addition to the compost heap. Its flowers are an alternative ingredient of 'QR' herbal compost activator and the roots of the plant improve fermentation of the compost heap when growing nearby. The leaves are used as an insect repellent, very effective when rubbed on the skin though they do impart their own unique fragrance. They can be powdered and placed amongst plants to act as a deterrent, or made into a spray. The dried flowering shoots are used to repel insects and rodents. The flowers are used in skin lotions, oils and ointments.

Elderberry is tolerant of salt-laden gales and can be grown as a shelter hedge in exposed maritime areas, although it is rather bare in the winter. It is an excellent pioneer species to use when re-establishing woodlands. It is very tough and wind-resistant, grows quickly and provides shelter for longer-lived and taller woodland species to establish. It will generally maintain itself in the developing woodland, though usually in the sunnier positions. A dye is obtained from the fruit and the bark. The bark of older branches and the root have been used as an ingredient in dyeing black. A green dye is made from the leaves and the berries yield various shades of blue and purple. They have also been used as a hair dye, turning the hair black. The blue colouring matter from the fruit can be used as a litmus to test if something is acid or alkaline; it turns green in an alkaline solution and red in an acid solution. The pith in the stems of young branches pushes out easily and the hollow stems thus made have been used as pipes for blowing air into a fire. They can also be made into musical instruments. The mature wood is white and fine-grained. It is easily cut and polishes well. Elderberry wood is highly valued by carpenters, as it has many uses including making skewers, mathematical instruments and toys.

Elderberry is a very easily grown plant, which tolerates most soils and situations. It grows well on chalk and in heavy clay soils, but prefers a moist loamy soil. It tolerates some shade but fruits better in a sunny position. It will also tolerate atmospheric pollution and coastal situations. The elderberry is very occasionally cultivated for its edible fruit. The sub-species S. nigra alba has white/green fruits that are nicer than the type species and are quite sweet raw. The elderberry also has a very long history of folk use, both medicinally and for a wide range of other uses.

Elderberry is a very valuable plant to have in the garden. The leaves often begin to open in winter and are fully open by spring. The leaves fall in autumn in exposed sites, later in sheltered positions. Late frosts can kill young stems but they are soon replaced from the ground level. Elderberry is very tolerant of pruning. It can be cut back to ground level and will regrow from the base. The flowers have a sweet, almost overpowering smell, which is not very pleasant when inhaled at close quarters as it has fishy undertones, but from a distance its musky scent is appealing. They are at their best after being dried. The fresh raw fruit is rich in vitamin C and has a rather rank taste. The fruit is typically cooked and used in pies, jams, jellies, sauces and bread. Elderberry is very resistant to the predations of rabbits. The flowers are very attractive to insects. The fruit is very attractive to birds and this can draw them away from other cultivated fruits.

Some cultivars have variegated or coloured leaves and are grown as ornamental plants. The following cultivars have gained the Royal Horticultural Society's Award of Garden Merit: S. nigra 'Aurea', S. nigra 'Laciniata' and S. nigra f. porphyrophylla 'Gerda' (syn. 'Black Beauty').

When propagating by seed, it is best to sow as soon as the seed is ripe in the autumn in a cold frame, when it should germinate in early spring. Cuttings of half-ripe wood are taken 7–10cm (4in) long with a heel in a summer. Cuttings of mature wood of the current season's growth are taken 15 – 20cm (8in) long with a heel, in late autumn. Division of suckers is possible in the dormant season.

As a Carbon Farming Solution plant, elderberry is highlighted as an industrial crop for dye and medicinal use.

American Elder

Sambucus nigra spp canadensis - (L.) R. Bolli

—Harvest —   —Edible Part —

Large   Z 3-9

American elder is native to eastern North America. The plant is a fast-growing deciduous shrub reaching 4m (13ft) in height. American elder can tolerate atmospheric pollution and strong winds, but struggles with maritime exposure. The Royal Horticultural Society currently lists American elder as Sambucus nigra var. canadensis.

American elder fruit is eaten raw or cooked and has a bittersweet flavour. The fruit is about 5mm (0.2in) in diameter and is borne in large clusters. Flowers are eaten raw or cooked and can be covered in batter and made into fritters. The flowers can be picked when unopened, pickled and then used as a flavouring in candies etc. They can also be soaked in water to make a drink. A pleasant tasting tea is made from the dried flowers. American elder can grow in semi-shade (light woodland) or full sun. Harvest flowers from early summer and fruit in the late summer.

As a Carbon Farming Solution plant, American elder is used as an industrial dye and medicinal crop. It is also a good contour hedgerow for agroforestry services.

American Elder

Sambucus nigra spp canadensis - (L.) R. Bolli
Family: Caprifoliaceae
Known Hazards: See Elderberry.
Natural Habitats: Rich moist soils along streams and rivers, woodland margins and waste ground.
Natural Range: Eastern N. America - Nova Scotia to Florida, west to Manitoba and Texas.
Hardiness Zones: USDA 3-9 . UK 3.
Size: A deciduous Shrub growing to 4m (13ft) by 4m (13ft)
Growth: Fast
Soil: Light (sandy), medium (loamy) and heavy (clay) soils and can grow in heavy clay soil. It prefers moist soil.
The plant can tolerate strong winds but not maritime exposure.
It can tolerate atmospheric pollution.
Soil pH: Acid, neutral and basic (alkaline) soils.
Light: Semi-shade or no shade.
Edibility Rating: 4
Medicinal Rating: 3
Other Uses Rating: 3
Carbon Farming: Agroforestry Services: Contour hedgerow. Industrial Crop: Dye; Medicinal. Management: Standard. Regional Crop.

spreading by suckers. This form is said to have the best fruit of the genus. It is a very hardy plant, succeeding as far north as S. Sweden and Nova Scotia. Japanese plum yew is dioecious, but female plants sometimes produce fruits and infertile seeds in the absence of any male plants. However, at least one male plant for every five females should be grown if the plants are grown for fruit and seed. Plants have also been known to change sex. Male cones are produced in the axils of the previous year's leaves, while female cones are borne at the base of branchlets.

Propagation is by seed and greenwood cuttings. The seed is sown as soon as it is ripe in a cold frame. Greenwood cuttings of terminal shoots are taken late in summer and kept in a humid cold frame, but propagating this way has a poor success rate.

Juniper

Juniperus communis - L.

—Harvest —   —Edible Part –

Large   4-10

Juniper is a coniferous evergreen shrub or tree with the most extensive geographical range of any woody plant. Its size is very variable, from a small prostrate spreading shrub, such as Juniperus communis compress, which only grows to 0.8m, to large trees.

The fruit has a soft, mealy, sweet, resinous flesh. It is usually harvested in the autumn when fully ripe and then dried for later use. It is used as a flavouring in sauerkraut, stuffing, vegetable paté etc., and is an essential ingredient of gin. According to one report, the aromatic fruit is used as a pepper substitute. The essential oil to be used as a flavouring is distilled from the fruit. Average yields are around 1%. The cones are about 4–8mm (0.3in) in diameter and take 2–3 years to mature. Some caution is advised when using the fruit. The roasted seed is a coffee substitute. Teas can be made by boiling the leaves and stems, or from the berries, giving a spicy gin-like flavour.

Juniper fruits are commonly used in herbal medicine, as a household remedy, and also in some commercial preparations. They are especially useful in the treatment of digestive disorders, and kidney and bladder problems. The fully ripe fruits are strongly antiseptic, aromatic, carminative, diaphoretic, strongly diuretic, rubefacient (produce redness of the skin by causing dilation of the capillaries and an increase in blood circulation), stomachic and tonic. They are used in the treatment of cystitis, digestive problems, chronic arthritis, gout and rheumatic conditions. Externally, it is applied as a diluted essential oil, having a slightly warming effect upon the skin, and is thought to promote the removal of waste products from underlying tissues. Fruits should not be used internally by pregnant women and can also increase menstrual bleeding. The essential oil is used in aromatherapy with the key term 'Toxin elimination'.

A decoction of the branches is used as an anti-dandruff shampoo. The essential oil is used in perfumes with spicy fragrances. In warmer climates, the tree yields the resin 'Sandarac' from incisions in the trunk. This is used in the production of a white varnish. The stems were at one time used as a strewing herb to sweeten the smell of rooms. The whole plant can be burnt as incense and fumigant. It was used during epidemics in the belief that it would purify the air and cleanse it of

Juniper

Juniperus communis - L.
Family: Cupressaceae
Known Hazards: Although the fruit of this plant is quite often used medicinally and as a flavouring in various foods and drinks, large doses of the fruit can cause renal damage. Juniper should not be used internally in any quantities by pregnant women. Diarrhoea with repeated use. Avoid in kidney disease. Do not use internally for more than 6 weeks.
Natural Habitats: Chalk downs in S. England but only where there is least sunshine and most rain, heaths, moors, pine and birch woods in the north of Scotland on acid peat, often dominant on chalk, limestone and slate.
Natural Range: Northern temperate zone, south to the mountains of N. Africa, Himalayas and California
Hardiness Zones: USDA 4-10. UK 2.
Size: Shrub growing to 9m (29ft)
Growth: Slow
Soil: light (sandy), medium (loamy) and heavy (clay) soils, prefers well-drained, dry or moist soil and can grow in heavy clay and nutritionally poor soils. Tolerate drought and maritime exposure.
Soil pH: acid, neutral and basic (alkaline) soils and can grow in very acid and very alkaline soils.
Light: It can grow in semi-shade or no shade.
Edibility Rating: 3
Medicinal Rating: 3
Other Uses Rating: 4
Forest Garden: Secondary layer; Sunny Edge; Dappled Shade; Ground Cover; Cultivated Beds.

infection. Fresh or dried juniper branches also make a good insect repellent. The bark is used as cordage and as a tinder. The wood is strong, hard, fragrant, very durable in contact with the soil and very close-grained, but usually too small to be of much use in construction. It makes an excellent fuel.

Many forms of this species are excellent ground cover plants for sunny situations. Try 'Depressa Aurea', 'Dumosa', 'Effusa' and 'Repanda' or 'Prostrata'.

Juniper is an easily grown plant succeeding in most well drained soils. It prefers a neutral or slightly alkaline soil and will grow well in heavy clay soils, chalky soils, hot, dry soils and poor soils. Juniper tolerates a pH range from 4 to 8. It likes light woodland but dislikes heavy shade. Once established it is very tolerant of drought. Although the fully dormant plant is cold-tolerant in colder climates, the young growth in spring can be damaged by late frosts. All parts of the plant are very aromatic. Juniper is a very polymorphic species that has a long history of culinary and medicinal use. It is frequently grown in the ornamental and herb garden, there is a vast range of cultivars of widely diverse habits. At least some forms tolerate maritime exposure. There is a thriving colony in an exposed position at Land's End in Cornwall, UK. The fruits take two to three years to ripen. Juniper is usually very slow growing, often only a few centimetres a year. It resists honey fungus, but rust sometimes attacks plants. Male and female plants must be grown if seed is required.

Juniper is propagated by seed, cuttings or layering. The seed requires a period of cold stratification. Juniper cuttings of mature wood are taken 5–10cm (4in) with a heel, in late summer, and planted out in the following autumn. Layering takes 12 months and is undertaken in late summer.

Lemon Verbena

Aloysia triphylla - (L'Hér.)Britton.

—Harvest —   —Edible Part —

Lemon verbena is a perennial shrub with lemon flavoured leaves. Originally cultivated for its oil, it was brought to Europe by the Spanish and the Portuguese in the 17th century. The leaves are occasionally cooked as spinach but are more commonly used as a flavouring in salads, fruit salads etc. A delicious and refreshing tea is made from the leaves. The leaves are often used to replace lemon and are common in Moroccan tea. The shrub is evergreen in warmer areas.

Lemon verbena has many medicinal uses including an antispasmodic, aromatherapy, febrifuge, sedative and as a stomachic. Its strongly lemon-scented essential oil has calming and digestive qualities. It has a gentle sedative action and a reputation for soothing abdominal discomfort. It has a mildly tonic effect upon the nervous system and helps to lift the spirits and counter depression.

Other uses include insecticide and potpourri. The essential oil from the leaves is extensively used in perfumery and is an effective insecticide in 1–2% concentration, repelling midges, flies and other insects. An average yield of 0.5% is obtained. There is some evidence that the use of the oil can sensitise the skin to sunlight, and so its use has mainly been replaced by the tropical plant lemongrass, Cymbopogon spp. The dried leaves retain their fragrance well, hence their use in potpourri.

Lemon Verbena is a very ornamental plant which succeeds in most moderately

Lemon Verbena

Aloysia triphylla - (L'Hér.)Britton.
Other Names: Lemon beebrush
Aloysia triphylla is synonym of Aloysia citriodora.
Family: Verbenaceae
Known Hazards: The essential oil from the plant might sensitise the skin to sunlight. Large doses of the tea can cause gastric irritation.
Natural Habitats: Fields and roadsides. Open scrub.
Natural Range: S. America - Argentina, Chile, Peru, Uruguay. Locally naturalized in the Mediterranean.
Hardiness Zones: USDA 7-11. UK 8.
Size: Shrub growing to 3m (9ft) by 3m (9ft)
Growth: Medium
Soil: light (sandy) and medium (loamy) soils and prefers a well-drained dry or moist soil.
Soil pH: Acid, neutral and basic (alkaline) soils.
Light: It can grow in semi-shade (light woodland) or no shade.
Edibility Rating: 4
Medicinal Rating: 3
Other Uses Rating: 3
Forest Garden: Sunny Edge; South or West Wall.

fertile soils if they are well-drained. It prefers a light soil, a sunny sheltered position, and a warm damp climate. Lemon verbena is only hardy in milder temperate areas. It can withstand about 10°C of frost and survives outdoors on a wall at Kew, UK. It survives most winters outdoors if growing in a suitable position, though it is often cut back to ground level and then re-sprouts from the base in late spring or early summer. Giving the roots a good, thick organic mulch will confer extra protection from winter cold. Any pruning is best carried out in the spring. Lemon Verbena is notably resistant to honey fungus.

Propagate Lemon Verbena from cuttings or seed. Cuttings of softwood are taken in early summer. Grow on for at least their first winter in a greenhouse if in colder areas, and plant out in late spring after the last expected frosts. The cuttings root quickly and easily, though there can be losses in the first winter. Cuttings of half-ripe wood are taken mid-summer and placed in a cold frame in colder areas. Grow them on for at least their first winter in a greenhouse and plant out in late spring after the last expected frosts.

Lemon Verbena has gained the Royal Horticultural Society's Award of Garden Merit.

Naranjilla

Solanum quitoense - Lam.

—Harvest —   —Edible Part —

Large   10-12

Naranjilla is an attractive, herbaceous, subtropical perennial shrub with large heart-shaped or oval-shaped leaves, which grows up to 3m (9ft) in height. It is short lived and can flower and fruit all year round. It is hairy or thorny. The bright orange fruits, produced in clusters on the trunk, are eaten raw or cooked, mainly used in sauces and preserves. Fruit is harvested late mid-spring to late-autumn. The flowers are pale violet. Naranjilla has no known medicinal value. It is propagated by seed sowing, cuttings, or grafting.

The fruit can be eaten raw or cooked and used in sauces and preserves. The tart yet sweet flavour is very refreshing, sometimes described as a combination of rhubarb and lime. The pulp is very juicy. The juice, which is rich in protein and minerals, is used in effervescent drinks and considered a delicacy in South America. The hairs on the skin of the fruit are removed before the fruit is eaten. The fruit is up to 5cm in diameter and is produced in clusters of 3–4 fruits.

Naranjilla does not do well in hot, lowland tropical areas. It appears to be tolerant of temperatures up to about 30°C but is intolerant of frost. It prefers a sunny position, but at lowland elevations it will often benefit from light shade. It can succeed in a range of soils so long as they are rich in organic matter. Its preference is for a light, fertile, well-drained soil, sheltered from strong winds with a pH in the range 6.5–7, tolerating between 5.8 and 8. Naranjilla was introduced into the Galapagos by settlers, and is considered to be invasive there. Naranjilla generally commences fruiting when about 10–13 months old. Annual yields of one to two tonnes of fruit per hectare are obtained. It can flower and fruit all year round. The flowers are hermaphrodite and usually self-fertile. Naranjilla is susceptible to attack by nematodes and other pests, limiting its cultivation. In recent years it has been hybridized with various species, especially with S. Sessiliflorum, with the result that most plants grown and served in Ecuador come from this hybrid. The hybrid can be distinguished from the true

Naranjilla

Solanum quitoense - Lam.
Other names: Quito Orange
Family: Solanaceae
Known Hazards: The fruits are covered in stinging hairs, though these are easily removed. Although providing many well-known foods for people, including the potato, tomato, pepper and aubergine, most plants in the family Solanaceae also contain poisonous alkaloids. Unless there are specific entries with information on edible uses, it would be unwise to ingest any part of this plant.(Handling plant may cause skin irritation or allergic reaction Plant has spines or sharp edges; use extreme caution when handling)
Natural Habitats: Montane forests.
Natural Range: Western S. America - Ecuador, Colombia, Peru.
Hardiness Zones: USDA 10-12. UK 10.
Size: Shrub growing to 2.5m (8ft)
Growth: Fast
Soil: light (sandy) and medium (loamy) soils and prefers well-drained moist soil.
Soil pH: Acid, neutral and basic (alkaline) soils.
Light: It can grow in semi-shade or no shade. The plant is not wind tolerant.
Edibility Rating: 4
Medicinal Rating: 0
Other Uses Rating: 0

Mahonia aquifolium

plant by the colour of its fruit pulp: pure Solanum quitoense has bright green fruit pulp, whereas the hybrids most often have yellowish or, at most, light greenish fruit pulp.

It is propagated by seed, cuttings, or grafting.

Oregon Grape

Mahonia aquifolium - (Pursh.)Nutt.

—Harvest —   —Edible Part —

Med   **Z** 4-8

Oregon grape is an excellent plant for shade and works well in woodland gardens. It is often seen in parks and green spaces because of its architectural form and winter interest. It is a favourite ornamental garden shrub. The fruit is almost as large as a blackcurrant and is produced in large bunches, so it is easy to harvest. It has an acid flavour, but it is rather nice raw, especially when added to porridge or muesli. There is relatively little flesh and a lot of seeds, though some plants have larger and juicier fruits. The cooked fruit tastes somewhat like blackcurrants. The fruit can also be dried and stored for later use. Flowers are eaten raw and can be used to make a lemonade-like drink.

Oregon grape is a North American native and the state flower of Oregon. It was used by several native North American Indian tribes to treat loss of appetite and debility. Its current herbal use is mainly in the treatment of gastritis and general digestive weakness, to stimulate the kidney and gallbladder function and to reduce catarrhal problems. The root and root bark are alterative, blood tonic, cholagogue, diuretic, laxative and tonic. Berberine, universally present in rhizomes of Mahonia species, has marked antibacterial effects and is used as a bitter tonic.

The inner bark of the stem and roots make a yellow/green dye. Dark green, violet and dark blue-purple colours come from the fruit. The leaves produce a green dye. This species can be grown as a low hedge and does not need trimming. Because of its suckering habit, it also makes an excellent dense ground cover plant, though it can be slow to become established.

Oregon grape is a very easy plant to grow, thriving in any good garden soil and tolerating dense shade under trees. It grows well in heavy clay soils and in dry soils if it is given a good mulch annually. It dislikes exposure to strong winds. It is hardy to about -20°C. Oregon grape is very tolerant of pruning and can be cut back into old wood if it grows too large and straggly. Spring is the best time to do this. Suckers are freely produced, with established plants forming dense thickets. Most plants grown under this name are casual hybrids with M. repens. This species is easily confused with M. pinnata, with which it also hybridizes. The flowers are delicately scented. Some named forms have been developed for their ornamental value. Cultivars have Royal Horticultural Society's Award of Garden Merit: M. × wagneri 'Pinnacle' (M. aquifolium × M. pinnata) and 'Apollo'. Landscape uses include borders, foundation, pest tolerant, massing, specimen and in a woodland garden.

Propagation is by seed, sucker division or leaf cuttings. Sow the seed as soon as it is ripe. It usually germinates in the spring. 'Green' seed (harvested when the embryo has fully developed but before the seed case has dried) should be sown

Oregon Grape

Mahonia aquifolium - (Pursh.)Nutt.
Other names: Hollyleaved barberry, Oregon Holly Grape, Oregon Holly
Family: Berberidaceae
Known Hazards: Barberry, goldenseal, oregon grape and other plants containing Berberine should be avoided during pregnancy and breastfeeding. Avoid if overactive thyroid gland. High doses cause vomiting, lowered blood pressure, reduced heart rate, lethargy, nose bleed, skin & eye irritation and kidney infection. Liquorice as Glycyrrhiza species nullify berberine effects.
Natural Habitats: Mixed coniferous woods to 2000 metres. It is found in woods and hedgerows in Britain.
Natural Range: Western N. America. Naturalized in Britain.
Hardiness Zones: USDA 4-8. UK 5.
Size: Shrub growing to 2m (6ft)
Growth: Fast
Soil: light (sandy), medium (loamy) and heavy (clay) soils and can grow in heavy clay soil. It prefers dry or moist soil.
Soil pH: acid, neutral and basic (alkaline) soils.
Light: It can grow in full shade, semi-shade or no shade.
Edibility Rating: 3
Medicinal Rating: 3
Other Uses Rating: 3
Forest Garden: Sunny Edge; Dappled Shade; Shady Edge; not Deep Shade; Ground Cover; Hedge.

as soon as it is harvested and germinates within six weeks. Division of suckers is done in spring. While they can be placed directly into their permanent positions, better results are achieved if they are potted up and put in a cold frame until established. Leaf cuttings are taken in the autumn.

Siberian Peashrub

Caragana arborescens -Lam

Siberian peashrub is a great food forest plant needing very little attention and producing edible seeds and seed pods for many years. Chickens, ducks and rabbits also enjoy the seeds. It is a fast-growing deciduous nitrogen-fixing shrub reaching 6m (19ft) in height. Leaves are alternate and compound with small leaflets and can be light to dark green. Small, yellow fragrant flowers bloom in early summer with pod fruits, containing many seeds, ripening in mid-summer.

The small, abundant seeds are eaten cooked. There are 4 to 6 seeds per pod with a bland flavour and best used in spicy dishes. The raw seed has a mild, pea-like taste, though it is unclear if it should be eaten in quantity when raw. The seed contains 12.4% of fatty oil and up to 36% protein. It is recommended as an emergency food for humans, and has the potential to become a staple crop in areas with continental climates. Young pods are cooked and used as a vegetable.

A fibre obtained from the bark is used for making cordage. A blue dye is obtained from the leaves. The plant can be grown as a hedge, it is quite wind-resistant and can also be planted in a shelterbelt. It has an extensive root system and can be used for erosion control, especially on marginal land. Because of its nitrogen-fixing capacity, it is valued as a soil-improving plant.

As a Carbon Farming Solution plant, Siberian peashrub is a staple protein crop managed as a standard or coppiced. Agroforestry uses include a living fence, nitrogen fixing, and a good windbreak. As an industrial crop it is a good biomass plant.

Siberian Peashrub

Caragana arborescens -Lam
Other names: Siberian Pea Tree,
Family: Leguminosae (previously Fabaceae)
Known Hazards: Reports that this plant contains toxins have not been substantiated.
Natural Habitats: River banks, pebbles, sands, open forests and forest edges, gully slopes and stony slopes.
Range: E. Asia - Siberia to Mongolia.
Hardiness Zones: USDA 2-7. UK 2.
Size: A deciduous Shrub growing to 6m (19ft)
Growth: Medium to fast
Soil: Light and medium soils, prefering well-drained dry or moist soil. Tolerate drought, poor soils, & strong winds.
Soil pH: Acid, neutral and very alkaline soils.
Light: It cannot grow in the shade.
Edibility Rating: 5
Other Uses: 4
Medicinal Rating: 1
It can fix Nitrogen.
Forest Garden: Sunny Edge; Hedge.
Carbon Farming: A Staple protein crop.
Agroforestry Services: Living fence; Nitrogen; Windbreak. Industrial Crop: Biomass.
Management: Coppice or Standard.

Littleleaf Peashrub

Caragana microphylla – Lam

Littleleaf peashrub is a pioneer leguminous shrub species for vegetation re-establishment growing to 1.5m (5ft) in boreal to warm temperate climates. It is suitable for dry conditions. It is an alternative peashrub to consider planting as a hedgerow, windbreak or as a fodder plant. The variety Caragana microphylla 'Mongolian Silver Spires' has bright, ferny silver leaves with a narrow, upright, arching habit. Seeds and seedpods can be harvested in the summer and autumn.

Littleleaf peashrub is a good Carbon Farming Solution plant that can be managed as a standard or coppiced. Agroforestry uses include nitrogen fixing, a contour hedgerow and a windbreak. It is also a good fodder plant.

Littleleaf Peashrub

Caragana microphylla – Lam
Family: Leguminosae (previously Fabaceae)
Hardiness Zones: USDA 5-9. UK 5.
Size: Shrub growing to 1.5m (5ft).
Growth: Fast
Soil: Suitable for: well-drained dry or moist light and medium soils. It can grow in nutritionally poor soil and tolerates drought & strong winds.
Soil pH: Acid, neutral and basic (alkaline) soils.
Light: It cannot grow in the shade.
Edibility Rating: 2
Other Uses Rating: 4
Forest Garden: Sunny Edge; Hedge.
Carbon Farming: Management: Standard or coppice. Agroforestry Services: nitrogen, contour hedgerow, windbreak. Fodder: bank.

Caragana microphylla

Peatree

Caragana brevispina -Royle. ex Benth.

—Harvest —   —Edible Part —

Large Z 5-9

Peatree is similar to C. arborescens but with larger, more bitter seeds. It grows very fast to 2.4m (8ft). It tolerates wind and drought and makes a good windbreak. The dense, spiny branches also make it an excellent hedging plant.

Siberian Peatree

Caragana boisii -Schneid

—Harvest —   —Edible Part —

Large Z 2-7

Caragana boisii is a smaller shrub, closely related to C. arborescens and with similar uses. It grows at a fast rate to 2m.

Pepino

Solanum muricatum - Aiton.

—Harvest —   —Edible Part —

Small Z 8-11

Peatree

Caragana brevispina -Royle. ex Benth.
Other names: Bebali kanda
Family: Leguminosae (previously Fabaceae)
Known Hazards: See Caragana arborescens.
Natural Habitats: Higher forests, in the undergrowth of fir and oak forests or in open glades on dry ridges from 1500 - 2700 metres.
Natural Range: E. Asia - N.W. Himalayas.
Hardiness Zones: USDA 5-9. UK 6.
Size: Shrub growing to 2.5m (8ft).
Growth: Fast
Soil: See *Caragana arborescens*
Soil pH: Acid, neutral and basic (alkaline) soils.
Light: It cannot grow in the shade.
Edibility Rating: 4
Medicinal Rating: 1
Other Uses Rating: 3
Forest Garden: Sunny Edge; Hedge.

Siberian Peatree

Caragana boisii -Schneid
Family: Leguminosae (previously Fabaceae)
Known Hazards: See Caragana arborescens.
Natural Habitats: Not known
Natural Range: E. Asia - China.
Hardiness Zones: USDA 2-7. UK 2.
Size: Shrub growing to 2m (7ft)
Growth: Fast
Soil: See *Caragana arborescens*
Soil pH: acid, neutral and basic (alkaline). Grows in very alkaline soils.
Light: It cannot grow in the shade.
Edibility Rating: 4
Other Uses Rating: 4
Forest Garden: Sunny Edge; Hedge.

Pepino or pepino dulce (sweet cucumber) is an evergreen shrub growing to 1m (3ft). It is grown for its sweet edible fruit similar to honeydew or rockmelon, with a juicy melon-like texture. Its sprawling habit makes it is an excellent ground cover plant to grow on a fence or trellis. The skin of some varieties has a disagreeable flavour. The fruit contains 35mg vitamin C per 100g, 7% carbohydrates and 92% water. The fruit is harvested just before it is fully ripe, in late summer to early winter, and will store for several weeks at room temperature. The fruit is about 10cm long (4in) and 6cm (2.4in) wide.

Pepino dulce succeeds in most well-drained soils in a sunny position. If the soil is too fertile, fruit production

will suffer due to excess vegetative growth. Plants require a pH above 6 in order to avoid disorders such as manganese toxicity or iron deficiency. Yields of 40–60 tonnes per hectare have been achieved. Plants are not very hardy in colder temperate regions, as they are cut to the ground by light frosts. Seedlings show no resistance to frost. Established plants are cut back at -3°C. However, in a warm position and given a good mulch, the roots can survive the winter and regrow from the base in the spring. Cuttings are exceedingly easy and can be overwintered in a greenhouse to provide fresh plants for the following year. Pepino dulce does not appear to have a sensitivity to day length. It can set fruit parthenocarpically (without fertilisation or seed being formed) but self-fertilisation or insect fertilisation greatly encourages fruiting. High temperatures, particularly above 30°C at flowering time, can cause the flowers to abort.

Propagation is by seed, cuttings and layering. Sow seed in early spring. Cuttings of half-ripe wood are taken in mid-summer and are very easy. In colder climates overwinter in a greenhouse and plant out after the last expected frosts. Layering is also easy.

Pigeon Pea

Cajanus cajan - (L.) Millsp

—Harvest —   —Edible Part —

Large   **Z** 9-12

Pigeon pea is an excellent fast growing permaculture plant with many uses, and is ideal as a pioneer plant when first starting a garden. It can be hard pruned to keep the plant low for harvesting. The pruned material makes an excellent mulch or is added to the compost pile. Pruning the top will release nitrogen from the roots into the soil to make it available to other plants. Pigeon pea is a woody perennial shrub that reaches only up to 4m high upon maturity if left unpruned. The plant is grown in the tropics and subtropics for various uses. It is damaged by frost and should be grown as an annual using fast-growing cultivars in colder climates. It is short-lived (up to five years), but new plants grow quickly. It is believed to be one of the earliest of cultivated plants, used for over 3,500 years. It has deep tap roots hence it can tolerate drought and poor soil conditions. Edible parts of pigeon pea are the seeds, seedpods, leaves and young shoots. Pigeon pea is as well known for its medicinal uses. Leaves are used as a treatment for coughs, bronchitis, diarrhoea, haemorrhages, sores and wounds. Diabetes and sore throats can likewise be treated using other plant parts of pigeon pea. Pigeon pea is planted as green manure. The stems are used as material in making baskets and in thatching. The wood is used in light construction. It can fix Nitrogen. It is a good fodder plant for cows, pigs and chickens.

Annual, medium and late cultivars are harvested in summer, while early and medium yielding cultivars can be harvested in winter. Very young seeds can be cooked and eaten like peas, going well in rice dishes. Mature seeds are dried, usually on the bush and harvested in winter, and added to soups and stews. They are small but flavourful. The seed may be used instead of soya bean to make tempeh or tofu, and can also be sprouted and eaten when about 25mm long. Seeds are high in protein and fibre while being low in fat. The seed is usually round or oval and up to 8mm in diameter. The seedpods are cooked. The unripe pods are eaten in curries. The pods are up to 10cm long and 14mm wide. The leaves and young shoots are cooked and used as a vegetable. They

Pepino

Solanum muricatum - Aiton.
Family: Solanaceae
Known Hazards: No specific mention of toxicity has been seen for this species.
Natural Habitats: Not known
Natural Range: S. America - Chile, Peru.
Hardiness Zones: USDA 8-11. UK 9.
Size: Shrub growing to 1m (3ft)
Growth: Fast
Soil: light (sandy), medium (loamy) and heavy (clay) soils and prefers well-drained moist soil.
Soil pH: acid, neutral and basic (alkaline) soils.
Light: It cannot grow in the shade.
Edibility Rating: 4
Forest Garden: Cultivated Beds.

Pigeon Pea

Cajanus cajan - (L.) Millsp
Other names: Puerto Rico Bean, Gandul, Dhal.
Family: Fabaceae
Natural Habitats: Not known in a truly wild situation.
Range: E. Asia - India.
Hardiness Zones: USDA 9-12. UK 10.
Size: Evergreen shrub growing to 4m (13ft)
Growth: Fast.
Soil: Well-drained, moist, light, medium or heavy soils. Tolerates drought & poor soil.
Soil pH: Acid, neutral and basic (alkaline) soils and can grow in very alkaline soils.
Light: It cannot grow in the shade.
Edibility Rating: 4
Medicinal Rating: 2
Other Uses: 4
Carbon Farming. A Staple protein crop. Agroforestry Services: Alley crop; Crop shade; Nitrogen; Windbreak. Fodder: Bank or Insect.

Siberian Apricot

Prunus sibirica – L.

—Harvest —   –Edible Part –

Large   **Z** *4-8*

Siberian apricot is a deciduous shrub, native to eastern China, Japan, Korea, Mongolia and eastern Siberia, growing to 3m (10ft). An edible oil resembling olive oil is obtained from the seed, and used as a substitute for almond flavouring. The fruit is eaten raw or cooked, and is a good size: about 25mm x 25mm (1in), and contains one large seed. The fruit is occasionally eaten but is sour and scarcely edible. The fruit seed is eaten raw or cooked and has a bitter taste. If the seed is too bitter do not eat it. Siberian apricot can grow in semi-shade (light woodland) or full sun. The fruit is harvested in early to mid-summer.

As a Carbon Farming Solution plant, Siberian apricot is a staple oil crop and an industrial oil crop.

Ebbing's Silverberry

Elaeagnus x ebbingei - Boom.

—Harvest —   –Edible Part –

Large   **Z** *5-9*

The fruit of Silverberry is a reasonable size, about 20mm (0.8in) long and 13mm (0.5in) wide, although it does have a large seed. The fully ripe fruit has a very rich flavour and is pleasant to taste with a slight acidity. The fruit should be deep red and very soft when it is fully ripe, otherwise it will be astringent. The flavour improves further if the fruit is stored for a day or two after being picked. The fruit ripens intermittently over a period of about six weeks from early to mid-spring. The seed is eaten raw or cooked. It can be eaten with the fruit though the seed case is somewhat fibrous. The taste is vaguely like peanuts.

Silverberry is a drought-resistant plant which, once established, can be grown on top of Cornish hedges (drystone walls with earth between two vertical layers of stones). It is very tolerant of shade and grows well under trees. It is very tolerant of maritime exposure. It is hardy to about -20°C. It can be deciduous in very cold winters. It fruits in early spring and has excellent potential as a commercial fruit crop in temperate zones. The fruit is of a reasonable size and when fully ripe is very acceptable for dessert. Not all plants bear many fruits, though many specimens have been seen that produce very heavy crops on a regular basis. Since this is a hybrid species, yields may be enhanced by growing a selection of cultivars or one of the parent plants

Prunus sibirica

Goumi Silverberry

Elaeagnus multiflora -Thunb
Other names: Cherry silverberry
Family: Elaeagnaceae
Known Hazards: None known
Natural Habitats: Thickets and thin woods in hills and on lowland, at elevations of 600 - 1800 metres.
Natural Range: E. Asia - China and Japan.
Hardiness Zones: USDA 5-9. UK 6.
Size: Shrub growing to 3m (9ft)
Growth: medium
Soil: light (sandy), medium (loamy) and heavy (clay). Prefers well-drained dry or moist soil and can grow in nutritionally poor soil. Tolerates drought. The plant can tolerate maritime exposure.
Soil pH: acid, neutral and basic (alkaline) soils.
Light: It can grow in semi-shade (light woodland) or no shade.
It can tolerate atmospheric pollution.
Edibility Rating: 5
Medicinal Rating: 2
Other Uses Rating: 3
Forest Garden: Sunny Edge; Dappled Shade; Hedge.

Japanese Silverberry

Elaeagnus umbellata - Thunb
Other names: Autumn Olive, Autumn Elaeagnus, Spreading Oleaster
Family: Elaeagnaceae
Hardiness Zones: USDA 3-7
Known Hazards: E. umbellata has the potential of becoming one of the most troublesome adventive shrubs in the central and eastern United States.
Natural Habitats: Thickets and thin woods in the lowland and hills
Range: E. Asia - China, Japan, and Himalayas.
Size: A deciduous Shrub growing to 4.5m
Growth: Medium
Soil: Light (sandy), medium (loamy) and heavy (clay) soils, prefers well-drained dry or moist soil and can grow in nutritionally poor soil. Tolerate drought. The plant can tolerate maritime exposure.
Soil pH: Acid, neutral and basic (alkaline) soils.
Light: It cannot grow in the shade.
Edibility Rating: 4
Medicinal Rating: 2
Other Uses: 4
Weed Potential: Yes
It can fix Nitrogen. It is noted for attracting wildlife.
Forest Garden: Sunny Edge; Dappled Shade; Hedge.
Carbon Farming: A Minor Global Crop. Agroforestry Services: Nitrogen; Windbreak. Fodder: Bank. Industrial Crop: Biomass. Management: Coppice or Standard.

nearby for cross-pollination. E. pungens is perhaps the best candidate for this and its cultivar E. pungens 'Variegata' has a good crop of fruit next to E. x ebbingei plants that are also laden with fruit. The cultivar E. x ebbingei 'Gilt Edge' is also probably a good pollinator. Other cultivars worth looking at are 'Salcombe Seedling', which is said to flower more abundantly than the type and 'Limelight', with a good crop of fruits even on small bushes. This species is notably resistant to honey fungus.

Goumi Silverberry

Elaeagnus multiflora -Thunb

—Harvest — —Edible Part — Large 5-9

Goumi is a low-maintenance, nitrogen-fixing, deciduous or semi-evergreen shrub or small tree. When ripe in early to late summer, the fruit is juicy and edible, with a sweet but astringent taste somewhat similar to that of rhubarb. For the best flavour, the fruit should be very ripe, when it turns soft and bright red. The skin of the fruit is thin and fragile, making it difficult to transport, thus reducing its viability as a food crop. On young shrubs, the fruit can be eaten by birds and older shrubs may need netting if this persists. The seed is also edible and similar to a sunflower seed in taste and texture. The fruit is well hidden in the shrub and is quite difficult to harvest without damaging the plant. Goumi is an excellent companion plant, when grown in orchards it can increase yields from the fruit trees by up to 10%. The small flowers are deliciously scented with a lilac-like smell, their aroma pervading the garden on calm days.

Japanese Silverberry

Elaeagnus umbellata - Thunb

—Harvest — —Edible Part — Large 3-7

Japanese Silverberry is a nitrogen-fixing deciduous shrub or small tree growing up to 4.5m (14ft) at a medium growth rate. The flowers are fragrant, blooming in the spring, with a lovely warm spice smell. Japanese Silverberry can grow in nutritionally poor soil and can tolerate drought and maritime exposure.

The red berries are juicy and pleasantly acid. The fruit is tasty raw and can be made into jams, condiments and preserves. It can be used instead of tomatoes in dishes. The fruit must be fully ripe to eat raw, otherwise it is quite astringent. The fruit contains about 8.3% sugars, 4.5% protein, 1% ash. The vitamin C content is about 12mg per 100g. Mature bushes in the wild yield about 650g of fruit over 2–3 pickings. The harvested fruit stores for about 15 days at room temperature. The fruit is about 8mm (0.3in) in diameter and contains a single large seed. The seed can be used raw or cooked and can be eaten with the fruit though the seed case is rather fibrous. Japanese Silverberry is noted for attracting wildlife. Berries will begin ripening from late summer and continue to bear fruit until late autumn.

Japanese Silverberry is a noted Carbon Farming Solution plant grown as biomass. It is managed as a standard or coppiced and fixes nitrogen, as well as acting as a windbreak.

Elaeagnus umbellata

Oleaster Silverberry

Elaeagnus angustifolia - L

—Harvest —   —Edible Part —

Large   Z 2-7

Oleaster Silverberry is a thorny shrub or small tree also called Russian olive, Persian olive or wild olive. The reddish-orange, oval fruit is about 10mm (0.4in) long and contains a single large seed. It ripens in autumn and is very popular with birds. The seed can be eaten with the fruit though the seed case is somewhat fibrous. The fruit must be fully ripe before it can be appreciated raw. If even slightly under-ripe it will be quite astringent. When cooked it is dry, sweet and mealy. It is used as a seasoning in soups and also prepared into jellies or sherbets.

The oil from the seeds is used with syrup as an electuary in the treatment of catarrh and bronchial affections. The juice of the flowers has been used in the treatment of malignant fevers. The fruit of many members of the genus is a very rich source of vitamins and minerals, especially in vitamins A, C and E, flavanoids and other bio-active compounds. It is also a fairly good source of essential fatty acids, which is fairly unusual for a fruit. It has other uses including essential oil, fuel, gum, as a hedge and for its wood.

Oleaster Silverberry can be grown as a hedge in exposed positions, tolerating maritime exposure. It is fast-growing and very tolerant of pruning, but is somewhat open in habit and does not form a dense screen. Because the plant fixes atmospheric nitrogen, it makes a hedge that enriches the soil rather than depriving it of nutrients. An essential oil obtained from the flowers is utilized in perfumery. A gum from the plant is used in the textile industry in calico printing. The wood is hard, fine-grained, used for posts, beams, domestic items and for carving. The wood is an excellent fuel.

Oleaster Silverberry is an easily grown plant requiring a position in full sun, growing very well in hot dry positions. It prefers a light sandy soil that is only moderately fertile, and succeeds in poor soils and dry soils. It succeeds in most soils that are well-drained, though it dislikes shallow chalk soils. It is very drought and wind resistant, and tolerates conditions of considerable salinity and alkalinity. It is a very hardy plant, enduring temperatures down to about -40°C. However, it prefers a continental climate and is apt to be cut back in severe

Oleaster Silverberry

Elaeagnus angustifolia - L
Other names: Russian Olive
Family: Elaeagnaceae
Known Hazards: None known
Natural Habitats: By streams and river banks to 3000 metres in Turkey.
Natural Range: Europe to W. Asia, as far north as latitude 55° in Russia.
Hardiness Zones: USDA 2-7. UK 2.
Size: Shrub growing to 7m (23ft)
Growth: medium
Soil: Suitable for: light (sandy), medium (loamy) and heavy (clay) soils. Prefers well-drained dry or moist soil and can grow in nutritionally poor soil. Tolerate drought. The plant can tolerate maritime exposure.
Soil pH: acid, neutral and basic (alkaline) soils and can grow in very alkaline and saline soils.
Light: It cannot grow in the shade.
Edibility Rating: 4
Medicinal Rating: 2
Other Uses Rating: 4
Forest Garden: Sunny Edge; Dappled Shade; Hedge.
Carbon Farming: Agroforestry Services: Nitrogen; Windbreak. Fodder: Bank. Industrial Crop: Biomass. Management: Coppice or Standard. A Minor Global Crop.

winters in colder temperate areas as the summer is not warm enough to have fully ripened the wood. This species is cultivated in N. Europe for its edible fruits. There are many named varieties available, some of which are thornless. Oleaster Silverberry fixes atmospheric nitrogen for the growing plant, but some can benefit other plants growing nearby. It is an excellent companion plant. When grown in orchards it can increase yields from the fruit trees by up to 10%. It is very tolerant of pruning, re-sprouting freely when cut to the ground. This species is notably resistant to honey fungus. The flowers are sweetly and heavily scented.

Propagation is by seed, cuttings and layering. The seed is sown as soon as it is ripe. It should germinate in late winter or early spring, though it may take 18 months. Stored seed can be very slow to germinate, often taking more than 18 months. Cuttings of half-ripe wood, 7–10cm (4in) with a heel, are taken in early summer. Cuttings of mature wood of the current year's growth, 10–12cm (4in) with a heel, are taken in late summer. The cuttings are rather slow and difficult to root, leave them for 12 months. Layering is possible in late summer; it takes about 12 months. Root cuttings are taken in the winter.

As a Carbon Farming Solution plant, Oleaster Silverberry can be used for nitrogen and as a windbreak for agroforestry services and as a fodder and a biomass industrial crop

Lemon Sumach

Lemon Sumach

Rhus aromatica - Aiton.
Other names: Fragrant sumac
Family: Rhus aromatica - Aiton.
Known Hazards: There are some suggestions that the sap of this species can cause a skin rash in susceptible people, but this has not been substantiated. See also notes in 'Cultivation Details'.
Natural Habitats: Dry rocks, sands and open woods, often on limestone.
Natural Range: Eastern N. America - Quebec to Florida, Indiana to Texas.
Hardiness Zones: USDA 3-9. UK 3.
Size: Shrub growing to 1.2m (4ft)
Growth: Slow
Soil: light, medium and heavy soils, prefering well-drained, dry to moist soil. Grows in nutritionally poor soil. Tolerates drought.
Soil pH: acid, neutral and basic (alkaline) soils.
Light: It cannot grow in the shade.
Edibility Rating: 4
Medicinal Rating: 2
Other Uses Rating: 2
Forest Garden: Sunny Edge; Cultivated Beds.

Rhus aromatica - Aiton.

— Harvest —   — Edible Part —   Medium   Z 3-9

Lemon sumach is a woody deciduous shrub, native to western North America, that grows to around 1.2m (4ft) at a slow rate. The fruit is small (about 5-7mm, 0.25in) with very little flesh, but it is easily harvested and when soaked for 10–30 minutes in hot or cold water makes a very refreshing still lemonade. The mixture should not be boiled since this will release tannic acids and make the drink astringent. The fruit can also be dried and ground into powder, then mixed with cornmeal and used in cakes, porridges etc. The leaves and stems have a citrus fragrance when crushed. Fruits ripen in late spring to early summer, and as late as early autumn in colder climates.

The leaves, root bark and fruit are astringent and diuretic. The leaves are used in the treatment of colds, stomach aches and bleeding. An infusion of the root bark and fruit is used in the treatment of diarrhoea and dysentery. The fruits have been chewed in the treatment of stomach aches, toothaches and gripe and used as a gargle to treat mouth and throat complaints. Some caution is advised in the use of the leaves and stems of this plant.

The leaves are rich in tannin (up to 25%) and can be collected as they fall in the autumn then used as a brown dye or as a mordant. The bark is also a good source of tannin. An oil extracted from the seeds attains a tallow-like consistency on standing and is used to make candles which burn brilliantly, though they emit a pungent smoke. The plant has an extensive root system and is sometimes planted to prevent soil erosion. The split stems are used in basket making.

Lemon sumach succeeds in well-drained, fertile soil in full sun but will tolerate poor soils. Established plants are drought resistant. Lemon sumach is a very hardy plant when fully dormant, enduring temperatures down to about -25°C, however, the young growth in spring is damaged by late frosts. Many of the species in this genus are highly toxic and can also cause severe irritation to the skin of some people, while other species, such as this one, are not poisonous. It is relatively simple to distinguish which is which. The poisonous species have axillary panicles and smooth fruits, while non-poisonous species have compound terminal panicles and fruits covered with acid crimson hairs. There is a particular low growing form, var. arenaria, that is found growing on dunes in the mid-west of N. America. Plants have brittle branches that are easily damaged in powerful winds. To some people, the plant has an offensive smell, for others the bruised leaves emit a delicious resinous scent. Male and female plants must be grown if the seed is required. This species transplants easily.

Propagation is by seed, cuttings or suckers. The seed is best sown as soon as it is ripe. Pre-soak the seed for 24 hours in hot water (starting at a temperature of 80–90°C and allowing it to cool) before sowing to leach out any germination inhibitors. This soak water can be drunk and has a delicious lemon flavour. Cuttings of half-ripe wood, 10cm (4in) with a heel, are taken in summer. Root cuttings 4cm (2in) long are taken in mid-winter and potted up vertically in a greenhouse. They are usually successful. Propagate by suckers in late autumn to winter.

Rhus typhina

Stag's Horn Sumach

Rhus typhina - L

—Harvest —   —Edible Part —

Large   4-8

Stag's horn sumach is a deciduous shrub growing up to 20 feet tall. It is a striking sight in winter when its bare branches carry purple spikes of fruit at their tips. These spikes, when soaked for a short while in cold water, yield a very refreshing drink, used in America as a lemonade substitute. Other members of this genus with fruits include R. aromatica and R. glabra.

Thymus vulgaris

Thyme

Thymus vulgaris - L.

—Harvest —   —Edible Part —

Small   5-8

Common thyme is a low growing shrubby evergreen herb popular in the kitchen and sometimes used as ground cover. It has attractive, edible, fragrant foliage which is slightly spicier than oregano and sweeter than sage. The leaves and flowering tops are eaten raw in salads, used as a garnish or added as a flavouring to cooked foods, going exceptionally well with mushrooms and courgettes. It is an essential ingredient of the herb mix 'bouquet garni'. It retains its flavour well in long slow cooking. The leaves can be used either fresh or dried. If the leaves are to be dried, the plants should be harvested in early and late summer just before the flowers open and the leaves should be dried quickly. An aromatic tea

Thyme

Thymus vulgaris - L.
Family: Lamiaceae or Labiatae
Known Hazards: A comment has been made in one report on medicinal uses that the plant should be used with caution. No explanation was given. It quite possibly refers to overuse of the essential oil. All essential oils, since they are so concentrated, can be harmful in large doses. Avoid if inflammatory disease of the gastrointestinal tract. Internal use contraindicated especially in pregnancy. Caution if sensitive to grasses. Dilute oil in carrier oil before topical use.
Natural Habitats: Dry slopes, rocks and maquis. Always found on clay or limestone soils.
Natural Range: S. Europe.
Hardiness Zones: USDA 5-8. UK 7.
Size: Shrub growing to 0.2m (0ft 8in)
Growth: Medium
Soil: light (sandy) and medium (loamy) soils, prefers well-drained soil and can grow in nutritionally poor soil. It prefers dry or moist soil. The plant can tolerate strong winds but not maritime exposure.
Soil pH: Neutral and basic (alkaline) soils.
Light: It cannot grow in the shade.
Edibility Rating: 4
Medicinal Rating: 3
Other Uses Rating: 5
Forest Garden: Ground Cover; Cultivated Beds. East, South or West Wall.

is made from the fresh or dried leaves which is pungent and spicy.

Common thyme has a very long history of folk use for a wide range of ailments. Uses include anthelmintic, antiseptic, antispasmodic, aromatherapy, carminative, deodorant, diaphoretic, disinfectant, expectorant, sedative and tonic. It is very rich in essential oils, and these are the active ingredients responsible for most of the medicinal properties. In particular, thyme is valued for its antiseptic and antioxidant properties, it is an excellent tonic and is used in treating respiratory diseases and a variety of other ailments. The essential oil is one of the most important oils used in aromatherapy; its keyword is 'bacterial'. It is used primarily in cases of exhaustion, depression, upper respiratory tract infections, skin and scalp complaints. The oil can cause allergic reactions and irritation to the skin and mucous membranes.

Other uses of common thyme include a deodorant, disinfectant, essential oil, fungicide, potpourri and as a repellent. Essential oil from the leaves is frequently used in perfumery, soaps, toothpaste, mouthwashes, medicinally etc. It has fungicidal properties and is also used to prevent mildew. It makes an attractive ground cover for a sunny position. Plants are best spaced about 30cm apart each way. The dried flowers are used to repel moths from clothing and the growing plant is said to repel cabbage root fly when grown near brassicas.

Common thyme is a beneficial plant in the garden and can be planted in a border, container, as a ground cover and in a rock garden. It prefers a light, dry calcareous soil and a sunny position. It will succeed in dry soils, poor soils and tolerates drought once established. Common thyme can be grown on old walls. It dislikes wet conditions, especially in the winter. A layer of gravel on the soil around it will help protect the foliage from wet soils. Common thyme is hardy to about -15°C, though it is even hardier when grown on old walls and in well-drained poor light soils. The cultivar 'Silver Queen', with white-margined leaves, has gained the Royal Horticultural Society's Award of Garden Merit. Common thyme flowers are rich in nectar and are very attractive to honey bees. Common thyme is an excellent companion for most plants.

Common thyme can be propagated by seed, cuttings and layering. The seeds are sown in spring for division in spring or autumn. Larger divisions can be planted out direct into their permanent positions. In the UK it has been found that it is best to pot up smaller divisions and grow them on in light shade in a greenhouse or cold frame until they are growing away well. Plant them out in the summer or the following spring. Cuttings of young shoots are taken 5–8cm (3in) long with a heel, in late spring. Cuttings of half-ripe wood are taken 5–8cm (3in) long with a heel, in mid-summer. Layering is also possible.

Trailing Abutilon

Abutilon megapotamicum - (Spreng.)A.St.-Hil.&Naudin.

—Harvest— —Edible Part–

 Med Z 7-10

Trailing Abutilon is a medium-size prolific flowering evergreen shrub growing to 2m. It has a flexible habit, with arching branches, large red calyces and small yellow lantern blooms. There are two forms of the species, one prostrate, making an excellent ground cover, the other upright. The prostrate form can be trained over arches or as a weeping standard.

The flowers of Trailing Abutilon are used as a vegetable. They have a pleasantly

EDIBLE SHRUBS

70+ TOP SHRUBS FROM PLANTS FOR A FUTURE

Increasing interest in food forests or woodland gardens reflects a growing awareness that permanent mixed plantings are inherently more sustainable than annual monocultures. They can safeguard and enrich soil ecosystems, enable plants to form mutually beneficial combinations, utilise layers both in the soil and above ground, and create benign microclimates which soften winds and recycle rain. Shrubs have an important role in food forests, occupying the highly productive layer between the canopy and the ground. Also, as perennial woody plants, shrubs help to draw down and store carbon from the atmosphere, a vital function to help combat damaging climate change.

Edible Shrubs provides detailed information, attractively presented, on over 70 shrub species. They have been selected to provide a mix of different plant sizes and growing conditions. Most provide delicious and nutritious fruit, but many also have edible leaves, seeds, flowers, stems or roots, or they yield edible or useful oil. The information here is based on practical experience and observation, and from a wide range of reputable sources. For each entry the descriptive text is augmented by summary information panels covering various attributes such as natural habitat, preferred soils, nutritional value, and potential uses within woodland garden designs.

We have included some more unusual species that may not be known to growers interested in a wider variety of food crops, or in more resilient designs for their plots. This book also has a quick reference table of the key characteristics of over 400 other perennials to help readers identify plants to meet specific requirements. Further details of all the plants described here are available from the PFAF Plants Database, which can be accessed free of charge at pfaf.org.

Plants For A Future

ISBN 9781791954949

9 781791 954949

sweet flavour and are delicious eaten raw. The flowers are produced from mid-spring until the autumn. They produce nectar all the time they are open, so if the plant is grown indoors and is not visited by pollinating insects, the sweetness increases the longer the flower is open.

Trailing Abutilon requires a sunny position or part day shade in fertile well-drained soil. It dislikes drought. It is only hardy in the mildest areas of Britain and similar climates, tolerating temperatures down to between -5 to -10°C when given the protection of a sunny wall. If it is cut back by cold weather, it will re-sprout from the base in the spring and can flower on the current year's growth. Dead-heading plants to prevent seeding can enhance longevity. Tip-prune young plants to promote a bushy habit; older plants can be cut back hard annually in spring if required. There are some named forms, selected for their ornamental value. There is a variegated form in cultivation, a result of infection by abutilon mosaic virus. Plants in this genus are notably resistant to honey fungus.

Propagate by seed and cuttings. Seed is sown in spring. Germination should take place within a few weeks. Once the seedlings are large enough to handle, prick them out into individual pots. In colder areas grow them on for at least the first winter in a greenhouse and plant out in late spring or early summer, after the last expected frosts. Take cuttings of young shoots in early summer. Plant outside in warm areas or grow on in the greenhouse for their first winter and plant out in spring after the last expected frosts. Take cuttings of half-ripe wood in mid-summer.

Tree Spinach

Cnidoscolus aconitifolius -(Mill.) I.M.Johnst

—Harvest —   —Edible Part —

Large   **Z** *9-11*

Tree spinach is a fast-growing tropical shrub or small tree of about 5m (16ft) in height. It is characterised by stinging hairs, pale trunk and alternate and simple leaves. It can grow in semi-shade (light woodland) or full sun, preferring moist soil but is drought tolerant. It is noted for attracting wildlife.

Young leaves and shoots are eaten as a cooked vegetable. The raw leaves contain potentially harmful cyanogenic glycosides which can break down to produce hydrogen cyanide upon tissue damage. They are only rarely eaten raw as fresh greens. Up to five raw leaves can be safely eaten a day. Cooking breaks down the glycosides, the time required to lower them to safe levels is about 15 minutes. The leaves, rich in protein, calcium, iron, carotene, riboflavin, niacin and ascorbic acid, have a good flavour and are boiled and used as a spinach substitute. They can be eaten them on their own or in combination with other vegetables in stews and soups. Traditionally leaves are immersed and simmered for 20 minutes and then served with oil or butter.

The leaves contain about 25% protein. A favourite drink in Yucatan (Mexico)

Trailing Abutilon

Abutilon megapotamicum - (Spreng.)A.St.-Hil.&Naudin.
Family: Malvaceae
Known Hazards: None known
Natural Habitats: Widely cultivated in the Tropics and not known in a truly wild situation.
Natural Range: S. America - Brazil.
Hardiness Zones: USDA 7-10. UK 8.
Size: Shrub growing to 2m (6ft)
Growth: Fast to Medium
Soil: light (sandy), medium (loamy) and heavy (clay) soils, preferring moist soil.
Soil pH: Acid, neutral and basic (alkaline) soils.
Light: It can grow in semi-shade (light woodland) or no shade
Edibility Rating: 4
Medicinal Rating: 0
Other Uses Rating: 0
Forest Garden: Sunny Edge; South or West Wall.

Tree Spinach

Cnidoscolus aconitifolius -(Mill.) I.M.Johnst
Other names: Tread Softly, Cabbage Star, Chaya
Family: Euphorbiaceae
Hardiness Zones: USDA 9-11. UK 10.
Known Hazards: The uncooked leaves contain cyanogenic glycosides that produce hydrogen cyanide upon tissue damage. The cooking time required to lower HCN to safe levels is about 15 minutes. Long-term contact with the white sap can cause skin irritation. The leaves of most members of this genus have stinging hairs; this species is, apparently, only lightly armed, though gloves should probably still be used when harvesting them.
Natural Habitats: Moist and dry thickets in open forest, often in open rocky localities, from sea level up to elevations of 1,300m.
Range: Central America - Panama to Mexico.
Size: Evergreen shrub growing to 5m (16ft)
Soil: Well-drained light (sandy), medium (loamy) and heavy (clay) soils. Prefers moist soil and can tolerate drought and poor soils.
Soil pH: Acid, neutral and basic (alkaline) soils including very acid and very alkaline soils.
Light: It can grow in semi-shade or no shade.
Growth: Fast
Edibility Rating: 4
Medicinal Rating: 3
Other Uses: 2
It is noted for attracting wildlife.
Carbon Farming: A staple protein crop.
Agroforestry Services: Crop shade; Living fence.
Management: Coppice or Standard. Minor Global Crop. Other Systems: Homegarden.

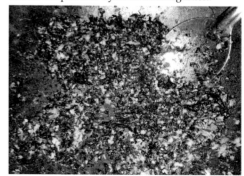

Cnidoscolus aconitifolius

is made by blending the raw leaves in sugar water with lemons, pineapple and other fruits. The drink is said to heighten virility. Leaves are available for harvesting all year.

Tree spinach is said to have many medicinal benefits, ranging from the ability to strengthen fingernails and darken greying hair. It is also used to cure alcoholism, diabetes, insomnia, skin disorders, venereal diseases, gout, scorpion stings and to improve brain function and memory. Numerous flavonoid compounds have been isolated from the leaves – most are kaempferol and quercetin glycosides. Tree spinach is known to contain proteolytic enzymes, which could explain the use of chaya sap for skin disorders.

As a Carbon Farming Solution plant, Tree spinach is an excellent staple protein crop that can be managed as a standard or coppiced. It provides good crop shade and can act as a living fence in agroforestry.

Wax Myrtle

Morella cerifera - (L.) Small. Myrica cerifera L. is a synonym of Morella cerifera (L.) Small.
Other names: Bayberry Wild Cinnamon.
Family: **Myricaceae**
Known Hazards: There is a report that some of the constituents of the wax are carcinogenic. Vomiting in large doses. Constituent myricadiol may cause salt retention and potassium excretion. Avoid if high blood pressure or kidney disease. Tannin constituents may cause gastrointestinal irritation and liver damage.
Natural Habitats: Thickets on sandy soil near swamps and marshes, also on dry arid hills in which situation it is often only a few cm tall.
Natural Range: South-eastern N. America. Possibly naturalized in S. England.
Hardiness Zones: USDA 7-11. UK 6.
Size: An evergreen Shrub growing to 9m (29ft)
Growth: Fast
Soil: light (sandy), medium (loamy) and heavy (clay) soils and prefers well-drained moist soil.
Soil pH: Acid and neutral soils.
Light: Semi-shade or no shade.
The plant can tolerate strong winds.
Edibility Rating: 3
Medicinal Rating: 3
Other Uses Rating: 4
Forest Garden: Sunny Edge; Dappled Shade; Hedge. It can fix Nitrogen.
Carbon Farming: Industrial Crop: Wax. Management: Standard.

Morella cerifera

Wax Myrtle

Morella cerifera - (L.) Small

—Harvest —   —Edible Part –

 Large **Z** 7-11

Wax myrtle is a fast-growing, nitrogen-fixing, evergreen shrub growing to 9m (29ft). It is native to the moist swampy woods and damp coastal areas of the southeast U.S. It can grow in semi-shade (light woodland) or full sun. The plant can tolerate strong winds but not maritime exposure.

The fruit is about 3mm (0.1in) in diameter with a large seed and is eaten raw or cooked. There is very little edible flesh, and the quality is poor. Leaves and berries are used as a food flavouring. They make an aromatic, attractive and agreeable substitute for bay leaves, and can be used in flavouring soups, stews etc. The dried leaves are brewed into a robust tea. Leaves are available all year and the berries in autumn and winter. Wax is made by boiling the berries and filtering.

As a Carbon Farming Solution plants, Wax myrtle is an excellent industrial wax crop managed as a standard.

Yeheb

Cordeauxia edulis -Hemsl

🍐🍐🍐🍐 💚💚💚💚 ⚔⚔⚔⚔

—Harvest — —Edible Part —

◯◯◯◯ ◯◯ ✕ ◯◯ 🖐 *Large* **Z** *10-12*

Yeheb is a woody evergreen legume of the arid semi-deserts of Ethiopia and Somalia growing to about 4m (13ft). It is highly valued for its nutritious nut, a staple food in drier areas and as a livestock forage plant during the dry season. The seeds taste similar to cashew nuts, almonds or chestnuts. In the Horn of Africa, it is the most important wild plant economically. As an important food and fodder plant, it has potential in other arid, hot regions.

As a Carbon Farming Solution plant, Yeheb is a staple crop used as a balanced carbohydrate. It can fix nitrogen and is a good fodder plant.

Yeheb

Cordeauxia edulis -Hemsl
Family: Leguminosae
Natural Habitats: Dry areas. Semi-arid scrub on coarse, deep red sands with a water table at 6.5 - 25m and at an elevation of 100 - 1,000m
Range: Northeastern tropical Africa - Somalia, Ethiopia.
Hardiness Zones: USDA 10-12. UK 10.
Size: Evergreen shrub growing to 4m (13ft).
Growth: Slow
Soil: Light (sandy) to medium (loamy). Prefers well-drained dry to moist soil and can grow in nutritionally poor soil. Tolerate drought.
Soil pH: Acid, neutral and basic (alkaline) soils.
Light: It cannot grow in shade.
Edibility Rating: 3
Medicinal Rating: 2
Other Uses: 4
Carbon Farming: Staple balanced carbohydrate. Cultivation: wild staple. Management: Standard.

Fodder: Bank. Agroforestry Services: nitrogen

Spanish Yucca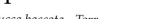

Yucca baccata - Torr.

🍐🍐🍐🍐 ❤💚💚💚💚 ⚔⚔⚔⚔⚔

—Harvest — —Edible Part —

Spanish Yucca or banana yucca (due to its banana-shaped fruit) is a drought tolerant, evergreen, succulent with attractive creamy white bell-shaped flowers.

The fully ripe fruit can be eaten raw, cooked or dried for winter use. It ripens in early to mid-autumn and remains green. The fruit is ripe if it is soft but not mushy when squeezed. Yucca fruit can be harvested before it is totally ripe and then allowed to ripen. Yucca fruit is large, fleshy, sweet and palatable, and was a staple food for several native North American Indian tribes. The ovoid fruit is about 17cm (6in) long and 7cm (3in) wide. The fruit baked in an oven is now considered to be a luxury by the native North American Indians. The cooked fruit can be formed into cakes and then dried for later use. Large quantities of the fruit has caused diarrhoea in people who are not used to it. The dried fruit can be dissolved in water to make a drink. Flower buds are cooked and have a soapy taste. The older flowers are best as they are rich in sugar. The flowers, harvested before the summer rains (which turn them bitter), have been used as a vegetable. Flowering stems are cooked. They are collected before the flowers open then roasted. Seed is also cooked. It can be baked and then ground into a powder and

Spanish Yucca

Yucca baccata - Torr.
Other names: Blue Yucca, Spanish Bayonet, Banana Yucca
Family: Agavaceae
Known Hazards: The roots contain saponins. Whilst saponins are quite toxic to people, they are poorly absorbed by the body and so tend to pass straight through. They are also destroyed by prolonged heat, such as slow baking in an oven. Saponins are found in many common foods such as beans. Saponins are much more toxic to some creatures, such as fish, and hunting tribes have traditionally put large quantities of them in streams, lakes etc in order to stupefy or kill the fish.
Natural Habitats: Rocky slopes, pinyon, oak, and juniper woodlands, grasslands at elevations of 400 - 2500m.
Natural Range: South-western N. America - Colorado to Texas, California and Mexico.
Hardiness Zones: USDA 6-11. UK 7.
Size: Shrub growing to 0.9m (3ft)
Growth: Slow
Soil: light (sandy), medium (loamy) and heavy (clay) soils, prefers well-drained soil and can grow in nutritionally poor soil. It prefers dry or moist soil and can tolerate drought.
Soil pH: acid, neutral and basic (alkaline) soils.
Light: It cannot grow in the shade.
The plant can tolerate strong winds but not maritime exposure.
Edibility Rating: 4
Medicinal Rating: 1
Other Uses Rating: 5
Forest Garden: Cultivated Beds; East Wall. South Wall. West Wall.
Carbon Farming: Agroforestry Services: Living fence. Historic Crop. Industrial Crop: Fibre. Management: Standard.

boiled. The tender crowns of the plants have been roasted and eaten in times of food shortage. The young leaves have been cooked as a flavouring in soups.

An infusion of the pulverized leaves has been used as an antiemetic to prevent vomiting. The fruits have been eaten raw as a laxative.

Spanish Yucca is used for basketry, brushes, fibres, needles, soap, string, waterproofing and weaving. A fibre obtained from the leaves is used for making ropes, baskets, paintbrushes and mats. The terminal spines have been used as needles. The dried leaves have been boiled with gum, hardened, ground into a powder then mixed with water and used to make baskets waterproof. The roots are rich in saponins and can be used crushed and then soaked in water to release the suds for use as a soap. It makes an excellent hair wash and can also be used on the body and for washing clothes. A solvent can also be obtained from the leaves and stems.

Spanish Yucca thrives in any soil but prefers a sandy loam and full exposure to the sun. It is hardier when grown on poor sandy soils. It prefers a hot, dry position, disliking heavy rain. Once established it is very drought resistant. In the plant's native environment, its flowers can only be pollinated by a particular species of moth, so hand pollination may be necessary. This can be done quite quickly and successfully using something like a small paint brush. Individual crowns are monocarpic, dying after flowering. However, the crown will usually produce some side shoots before it dies that will grow on to flower in later years. Members of this genus seem to be immune to the predations of rabbits.

Spanish Yucca is used in garden borders, massing and as a specimen. It also grows well in pots, although flowering will be restricted. It has attractive, fragrant flowers.

Propagation is by seed, root or division. Seed is sown in spring. Pre-soaking the seed for 24 hours in warm water may reduce the germination time. It usually germinates within one or two months if kept at a temperature of 20°C. Take root cuttings in late winter or early spring. Lift them in spring and remove small buds from the base of stem and rhizomes. Dip in dry wood ashes to stop any bleeding and plant in sandy soil in pots until established. Division of suckers can be done in late spring. Larger divisions can be planted out direct into their permanent positions. In the UK it has been found that it is best to pot up smaller divisions and grow them on in light shade in a greenhouse or cold frame until they are growing away well. Plant out in the following spring.

As a Carbon Farming Solution plant, Spanish Yucca can be used as a living fence and as an industrial fibre crop.

Spoonleaf Yucca

Yucca filamentosa -L

—Harvest —   —Edible Part —

Spoonleaf Yucca is an evergreen shrub which grows to about two and a half feet tall. It is a hardy plant which brings a sub-tropical appearance to the garden. It requires a sunny position and well-drained soil. In its native habitat, the flowers of this plant can only be pollinated by a specially adapted species of insect, so to produce fruits in colder temperate areas the flowers must be hand pollinated. Apart from this it is a very easy plant to grow, and the fruit is said to be a date substitute, eaten raw or dried for winter use. Harvest the fruit in autumn. Other uses for this plant include a fibre made from the leaves used to make ropes etc. and a soap obtained by boiling the roots. The flowers are said to be edible.

Spoonleaf Yucca

Yucca filamentosa -L
Other names: Adam's needle, Desert Candle, Needle or St. Peter's Palm
Family: Agavaceae
Known Hazards: See Spanish Bayonet
Natural Habitats: Sand dunes, waste ground and pine forests along the coastal plain
Natural Range: South-eastern N. America - Southern New Jersey to Florida. Naturalized in S. Europe.
Hardiness Zones: USDA 4-10. UK 4.
Size: An evergreen Shrub growing to 1.2m (4ft)
Growth: Medium
Soil: Light (sandy), medium and heavy (clay). Prefers well-drained, dry or moist soil and can grow in nutritionally poor soil. Tolerates drought.
Soil pH: Acid, neutral and basic (alkaline) soils.
Light: Semi-shade or no shade.
The plant can tolerate strong winds but not maritime exposure.
Edibility Rating: 3
Medicinal Rating: 1
Other Uses Rating: 4
Forest Garden: Cultivated Beds.

The PFAF Database

On the pfaf.org website you can search for over 7000 edible and medicinal plants using a number of search criteria including: common and Latin names, keyword, family, habitat and use (medicinal, edible or other).

Search techniques include:

- search by name

- search by keyword

- you can browse plants common and Latin names by alphabetical letter

- you can browse plants by their family, habitat and use (medicinal, edible or other)

- you can search for a plant by its use, for example whether it can be used for:

edible: e.g. coffee, chocolate, gelatine, oil

medicinal: e.g. acrid, antacid, antibiotic

other: e.g. alcohol, beads, bottles, fencing, fuel

special uses: e.g. nitrogen fixer, hedge

You can do a more detailed search using the Search Properties section. This allows you to search for a number of plant features at once. For example, you might want to search for a plant that needs a light sandy soil, that is between 1m and 5m high, and likes shade - the database will then present a list of plants that have all three of these features.

A Carbon Farming Search

Since 2017 Plants For A Future have been working on a project called *The Carbon Farming Solution* - a collection of plants that can be a critical part of the solution to climate problems. These are new plants to the PFAF database identified while researching and adding new tropical plants and also featuring in Eric Toensmeier excellent book *Carbon Farming Solution: A Global Toolkit of Perennial Crops and Regenerative Agriculture Practices for Climate Change Mitigation and Food Security.*

The PFAF database focuses on perennial plants for our gardens that can replace annual crops and help towards carbon sequestration and climate change mitigation. A number of these perennials are suited to large-scale farming. The database search on the homepage (pfaf.org) includes the ability to search carbon farming plants. Search criteria include:

Types of crop management. Non-destructive management systems for example standard, coppiced, hay and fodder.

Staple Crops. Foods that are a dominant part of people's diets in different parts of the world. Staple crops are used for protein, protein-oil, carbohydrates, oil, and sugar.

Industrial crops. Non-food uses: biomass, hydrocarbon, medicine, oil, fibre etc.

Agroforestry crops. Nitrogen, shade, windbreaks, understorey legume etc.

Fodder crops. Bank, pasture, pod etc.

On the individual plant pages, we have also included the cultivation status of each plant. Plants are divided into nine cultivation status categories ranging from global perennial staples and industrial crops to wild perennial staples. For more information on the categories, please visit: pfaf.org/user/CarbonFarmingSolution.html

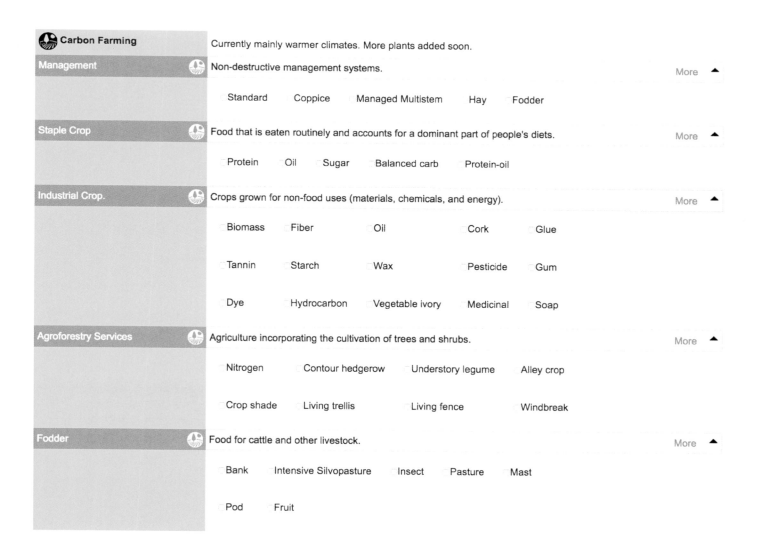

Plant Species Matrix: Additional Plants

	Common Name	USDA Hardiness	UK Hardiness	Height (m)	Edibility	Medicinal	Other Uses	Growth	Soil	Light	Moisture	pH
Abutilon ochsenii		7 to 10	8	4	3	0	0		LMH	SN	M	ANB
Abutilon pictum	Abutilon, Parlour Maple, Flowering Maple, Spotted	8 to 10	9	5	3	0	0	M	LMH	SN	M	ANB
Abutilon species		7 to 10	8	3	3	0	0		LMH	SN	M	ANB
Abutilon vitifolium		7 to 10	8	8	3	0	0		LMH	SN	M	ANB
Abutilon x hybridum	Chinese Lantern, Flowering Maple	9 to 11	8	3	3	0	0	F	LMH	SN	M	ANB
Abutilon x milleri	Trailing Abutilon	7 to 10	8	3	3	0	0		LMH	SN	M	ANB
Abutilon x suntense		7 to 10	8	8	3	0	0	F	LMH	SN	M	ANB
Amelanchier alnifolia cusickii	Cusick's Serviceberry		2	3	4	1	0		LMH	SN	M	AN
Amelanchier alnifolia semiintegrifolia	Pacific Serviceberry		2	3	5	1	1	S	LMH	SN	M	AN
Amelanchier bartramiana	Oblongfruit serviceberry	4 to 8	5	3	3	0	0		LMH	SN	M	AN
Amelanchier basalticola	Dwarf Service-berry	4 to 8	5	3	4	0	0		LMH	SN	M	AN
Amelanchier confusa		4 to 8	5	3	5	0	0		LMH	SN	M	AN
Amelanchier humilis	Low serviceberry	4 to 8	4	1.8	3	0	0		LMH	SN	M	ANB
Amelanchier intermedia	June berry,	4 to 8	4	6	3	0	0		LMH	SN	M	AN
Amelanchier laevis	Allegheny Shadberry, Allegheny serviceberry, Smooth Serviceberry	5 to 8	4	9	5	1	2	M	LMH	SN	M	AN
Amelanchier lamarckii	Apple Serviceberry	3 to 3	4	6	5	0	0		LMH	SN	M	AN
Amelanchier pallida	Pale Serviceberry		0	4	3	1	0		LMH	SN	M	AN
Amelanchier sanguinea	Roundleaf Serviceberry, GaspÈ serviceberry	4 to 8	4	3	3	0	0			SN	DM	ANB
Amelanchier spicata		4 to 8	4	2	3	0	0		LMH	SN	M	AN
Amelanchier stolonifera	Quebec Berry, Running serviceberry	4 to 8	4	1.5	5	1	0		LMH	SN	DM	AN
Amelanchier utahensis	Utah Serviceberry, Coville's serviceberry	3 to 7	3	5	3	1	2		LMH	SN	DM	AN
Amelanchier weigandii		5 to 9	6	5	3	0	0		LMH	SN	M	ANB
Amelanchier x grandiflora	Apple Serviceberry	4 to 7	4	6	5	0	0	S	LMH	SN	M	AN
Amomyrtus luma	Luma, Chilean guava,		0	7.5	3	0	0		LMH	N	DM	ANB
Arctostaphylos manzanita	Manzanita, Whiteleaf manzanita, Konocti manzanita, Contra Costa manzanita, Roof's manzanita, Wieslan	7 to 10	8	2	3	1	3		LM	SN	DM	A
Arctostaphylos patula	Greenleaf Manzanita	5 to 9	6	2	3	1	1		LM	SN	M	A
Arctostaphylos stanfordiana	Stanford's manzanita, Rincon manzanita	5 to 9	6	1.5	3	0	1		LM	SN	DM	A
Arctostaphylos tomentosa	Downy Manzanita, Woollyleaf manzanita, Brittleleaf manzanita, Dacite manzanita, Rosy manzanita, San	7 to 10	8	1.5	3	3	3		LM	SN	M	A
Arctostaphylos uva-ursi	Bearberry	4 to 8	4	0.1	3	4	4	M	LM	FSN	M	ANB
Aristotelia chilensis	Macqui	7 to 10	8	3	3	1	0		LMH	N	M	AN
Artemisia tridentata	Sage Brush, Big sagebrush, Bonneville big sagebrush	4 to 10	8	2.5	3	2	5		LM	N	DM	ANB
Asimina triloba	Papaw	5 to 8	5	4.5	4	2	2	F	M	N	M	ANB
Aspalathus linearis	Rooibos	8 to 11	9	2	3	3	0		LM	N	DM	AN
Astragalus massiliensis		5 to 9	6	0.3	3	0	3		LM	N	D	ANB
Astroloma humifusum	Cranberry Heath	7 to 10	8	0.1	3	0	0		LMH	N	DM	ANB
Astroloma pinifolium	Pine Heath	7 to 10	8	1	3	0	0		LM	N	DM	ANB
Atriplex canescens	Grey Sage Brush, Fourwing saltbush	6 to 9	7	1.8	4	1	3		LM	N	DM	ANB
Atriplex confertifolia	Shadscale, Shadscale saltbush	6 to 9	7	1.8	4	1	0		LM	N	DM	ANB
Atriplex lentiformis	Quail Bush, Big saltbush, Quailbush,	7 to 10	8	3	3	1	2		LM	N	DM	ANB
Atriplex nummularia	Giant Saltbush, Bluegreen saltbush	7 to 10	8	3.5	3	0	0		LM	N	DM	ANB
Atriplex nuttallii	Nuttall's Saltbush	5 to 9	6	0.9	4	0	0		LM	N	DM	ANB
Azorina vidalii		8 to 11	9	0.3	3	0	0		LM	N	DM	ANB
Baccharoides hymenolepis	Baccharoides	10 to 12	9	4	4	2	3	F	LMH	N	M	ANB
Berberis aggregata	Salmon Barberry	5 to 9	6	1.5	3	2	1	M	LMH	SN	DM	ANB
Berberis angulosa		5 to 9	6	1	3	2	1		LMH	SN	DM	ANB
Berberis asiatica	Chutro, Rasanjan (Nep); marpyashi (Newa); Daruharidra, Darbi (Sans)	7 to 10	8	3.5	4	3	2	M	LMH	FSN	DM	ANB

Growth: S = slow M = medium F = fast. **Soil:** L = light (sandy) M = medium H = heavy (clay)

pH: A = acid N = neutral B = basic (alkaline) **Light:** F = full shade S = semi-shade N = no shade. **Moisture:** D = dry M = Moist We = wet Wa = water

Scientific name	Common name											
Berberis buxifolia	Magellan Barberry	4 to 8	5	2.5	4	2	3		LMH	SN	DM	ANB
Berberis canadensis	Allegheny Barberry, American barberry	4 to 8	5	1.8	3	2	1	M	LMH	SN	DM	ANB
Berberis cooperi			0	1.5	3	2	1		LMH	SN	M	ANB
Berberis darwinii	Darwin's Barberry, Darwin's berberis	7 to 9	7	3	4	2	3	M	LMH	SN	M	ANB
Berberis georgii	Barberry	3 to 7	3	3	3	2	0	M	LMH	SN	DM	ANB
Berberis lycium		5 to 9	6	3	3	3	0	M	LMH	SN	DM	ANB
Berberis rubrostilla		5 to 9	6	1.5	3	2	0		LMH	SN	DM	ANB
Berberis vulgaris	European Barberry, Common barberry	3 to 7	3	3	3	3	4	M	LMH	SN	DM	ANB
Berberis wilsoniae		5 to 9	6	1	3	2	1		LMH	SN	DM	ANB
Berberis x carminea		5 to 9	6	2	3	2	1	M	LMH	SN	M	ANB
Berberis x lologensis		5 to 9	6	2.5	3	2	1	M	LMH	SN	M	ANB
Berberis x stenophylla		4 to 8	5	2.5	3	2	3	M	LMH	SN	M	ANB
Boscia senegalensis	Aizen, Boscia	10 to 12	10	8	4	2	3	M	LMH	FSN		ANB
Calycanthus floridus	Carolina Allspice, Eastern sweetshrub, Strawberry Bush, Sweetshrub, Carolina Allspice	5 to 10	5	2.7	3	2	2	M	LM	SN	M	ANB
Calycanthus occidentalis	Californian Allspice, Western sweetshrub	6 to 9	7	3	3	1	2		LM	SN	M	ANB
Camellia japonica	Camellia, Common Camellia, Japanese Camellia	7 to 9	7	10	3	2	2	S	LM	FSN	M	AN
Camellia reticulata	To-tsubaki	7 to 10	8	10	3	0	1		LM	SN	M	AN
Camellia sasanqua	Camellia, Sasanqua camellia	7 to 9	8	3	3	1	4	S	LM	SN	M	AN
Camellia sinensis	Tea Plant, Assam tea, Tea Tree Camellia	7 to 9	8	4	4	4	3	S	LM	S	M	AN
Camellia sinensis assamica	Tea Plant, Assam Tea	8 to 10	9	10	4	4	3	S	LMH	SN	M	AN
Capsicum chinense	Bonnet Pepper, Chinese capsicum	10 to 12	10	1.5	3	4	1	F	LMH	N	M	ANB
Caragana fruticosa	Siberian Peashrub,		2	2	3	0	5	F	LM	N	DM	ANB
Castanea alnifolia	Bush Chinkapin	6 to 9	7	1	3	0	2		LMH	N	DM	AN
Castanea pumila ashei	Chinquapin	6 to 9	7	5	4	1	2		LMH	N	DM	AN
Castanea x neglecta	Chinknut	4 to 8	5	4	3	0	3	S	LMH	N	DM	AN
Ceanothus americanus	New Jersey Tea, Wild Snowball	4 to 9	4	1.2	3	3	3	F	LM	SN	DM	ANB
Cephalotaxus fortunei	Chinese Plum Yew	6 to 9	7	6	5	1	3	S	LMH	FSN	M	ANB
Cephalotaxus harringtonia drupacea	Japanese Plum Yew	6 to 9	7	5	5	0	3	S	LMH	FS	M	ANB
Cephalotaxus harringtonia koreana	Korean Plum Yew	6 to 9	7	1.5	5	0	3	S	LMH	FS	M	ANB
Cephalotaxus harringtonia nana	Japanese Plum Yew	6 to 9	7	2	5	0	3	S	LMH	FS	M	ANB
Cephalotaxus lanceolata	Yunnan Plum Yew	7 to 10	8	8	4	0	2	S	LMH	FSN	M	ANB
Cephalotaxus oliveri		7 to 10	8	3	3	0	4	S	LMH	FSN	M	ANB
Cephalotaxus sinensis	Chinese Plum Yew	6 to 9	7	5	4	1	3	S	LMH	FS	M	ANB
Cercis occidentalis	Western Redbud, California Redbud	5 to 9	7	4.5	3	0	0	M	LM	SN	DM	ANB
Chaenomeles cathayensis	Chinese Quince	4 to 8	5	3	4	2	3		LMH	SN	M	ANB
Chaenomeles japonica	Dwarf Quince, Maule's quince, Japanese Flowering Quince	5 to 8	5	1	3	0	3	M	LMH	FSN	M	ANB
Chaenomeles x superba	Dwarf Quince, Flowering Quince	5 to 8	5	1	3	0	3	F	LMH	FSN	M	ANB
Citrus limon	Lemon	8 to 11	9	3	4	5	5	M	MH	N	M	ANB
Citrus x meyeri	Lemon	8 to 11	9	3	3	5	5	M	MH	N	M	ANB
Comptonia peregrina	Sweet Fern	3 to 6	4	1.5	3	3	3	M	LM	SN	DM	A
Comptonia peregrina asplenifolia	Sweet Fern	4 to 8	4	1.2	3	3	3		LM	SN	DM	A
Cornus officinalis	Shan Zhu Yu, Asiatic dogwood, Japanese Cornel Dogwood	5 to 8	6	10	4	3	0	M	LMH	SN	M	ANB
Corylus cornuta	Beaked Hazel, California hazelnut, Turkish Filbert, Turkish Hazel	4 to 7	4	3	3	1	3		LMH	SN	M	ANB
Corylus maxima	Filbert, Giant filbert	4 to 8	5	6	5	0	5		LMH	SN	M	ANB
Corylus sieboldiana mandschurica	Hairy hazel, Japanese hazelnut,	5 to 9	6	4.5	3	0	1		LMH	SN	M	ANB
Crataegus aestivalis	Eastern Mayhaw, May hawthorn, Mayhaw, Apple Hawthorn	6 to 11	4	9	3	2	5	M	LMH	SN	MWe	ANB
Crataegus anomala	Arnold hawthorn	4 to 8	5	5	3	2	3		LMH	SN	MWe	ANB
Crataegus baroussana	Tejocote		0	2	4	2	2		LMH	SN	MWe	ANB
Crataegus caesa		6 to 9	7	3	4	2	2		LMH	SN	MWe	ANB

Plant Species Matrix: Additional Plants

Species	Common name	Zone						Growth	Soil	Light	Moisture	pH
Crataegus cuneata	Sanzashi, Chinese hawthorn	5 to 9	6	15	3	3	3		LMH	SN	MWe	ANB
Crataegus durobrivensis	Caughuawaga Hawthorn	4 to 8	5	5	4	2	2		LMH	SN	MWe	ANB
Crataegus elongata			0	4	4	2	2		LMH	SN	MWe	ANB
Crataegus festiva		6 to 9	7	3	5	2	2		LMH	SN	MWe	ANB
Crataegus flabellata	Fanleaf hawthorn	4 to 8	4	6	3	2	3		LMH	SN	MWe	ANB
Crataegus flava	Summer Haw, Yellowleaf hawthorn	5 to 9	6	8	3	2	3		LMH	SN	DMWe	ANB
Crataegus intricata	Copenhagen hawthorn	4 to 8	5	3	3	2	3		LMH	SN	MWe	ANB
Crataegus laevigata	Midland Hawthorn, Smooth hawthorn, English Hawthorn	4 to 8	5	6	3	5	5	M	LMH	FSN	MWe	ANB
Crataegus meyeri			0	4	3	2	3		LMH	SN	MWe	ANB
Crataegus monogyna	Hawthorn, Oneseed hawthorn	4 to 8	5	6	3	5	3	M	LMH	SN	MWe	ANB
Crataegus opaca	Western Mayhaw	4 to 8	4	9	3	2	3	M	LMH	SN	MWe	ANB
Crataegus pedicellata	Scarlet Haw, Scarlet hawthorn	4 to 8	5	7	5	2	2		LMH	SN	MWe	ANB
Crataegus pedicellata gloriosa	Scarlet Haw	4 to 8	5	7	3	2	3		LMH	SN	MWe	ANB
Crataegus songorica			0	4.5	3	2	3		LMH	SN	MWe	ANB
Crataegus succulenta	Fleshy hawthorn	4 to 8	4	6	4	2	2		LMH	SN	DMWe	ANB
Crataegus szovitskii			0	0	3	2	3		LMH	SN	MWe	ANB
Crataegus x grignonensis		4 to 8	5	4	3	2	3		LMH	SN	MWe	ANB
Decaisnea fargesii	Blue Sausage Fruit	4 to 8	5	4	3	0	0	M	LMH	SN	M	ANB
Dovyalis abyssinica	Abyssinian Gooseberry	10 to 12	10	6	4	2	2		LMH	N	M	AN
Drimys lanceolata	Mountain Pepper	7 to 10	8	4.5	3	1	4	S	LM	S	M	AN
Drimys winteri	Winter's Bark	7 to 10	8	7.5	3	2	3		LM	S	M	AN
Elaeagnus commutata	Silverberry		2	3	3	2	4		LMH	N	DM	ANB
Elaeagnus cordifolia			0	4	5	2	3	M	LMH	FSN	DM	AN
Elaeagnus glabra	Goat nipple	7 to 10	8	6	4	2	3	M	LMH	FSN	DM	AN
Elaeagnus latifolia	Bastard Oleaster	8 to 11	9	3	3	2	2	M	LMH	N	DM	ANB
Elaeagnus macrophylla		6 to 9	7	3	5	2	3	M	LMH	FSN	DM	ANB
Elaeagnus multiflora ovata	Goumi	5 to 9	6	3	5	2	3	M	LMH	SN	DM	ANB
Elaeagnus orientalis	Trebizond Date	4 to 8	4	12	4	2	2	M	LMH	N	DM	ANB
Elaeagnus parvifolia	Autumn olive	3 to 7	3	4.5	4	2	2	M	LMH	N	DM	ANB
Elaeagnus pungens	Elaeagnus, Thorny olive, Thorny Elaeagnus, Oleaster, Silverberry, Silverthorn, Pungent Elaeagnus	6 to 10	7	4	5	2	3	M	LMH	FSN	DM	ANB
Elaeagnus umbellata	Autumn Olive	3 to 7	3	4.5	4	2	3	M	LMH	N	DM	ANB
Elaeagnus x reflexa		6 to 9	7	4.5	3	2	4	M	LMH	FSN	DM	ANB
Eleutherococcus sieboldianus	Ukogi, Five Leafed Aralia	4 to 8	4	3	3	0	2	S	LMH	SN	M	ANB
Empetrum nigrum	Crowberry, Black crowberry, Black Crowberry	3 to 8	3	0.3	3	2	1		LMH	SN	M	AN
Ephedra nevadensis	Mormon Tea, Nevada jointfir	5 to 9	6	1.2	3	3	0		LM	N	DM	ANB
Eugenia brasiliensis	Grumichama, Brazilian Plum	9 to 12	10	8	4	2	2	S	LMH	SN	M	AN
Eugenia uniflora	Brazil Cherry	10 to 12	10	6	4	3	3	S	LMH	SN	DM	AN
Fortunella japonica	Round Kumquat	8 to 11	9	2.5	3	1	2		LMH	SN	M	ANB
Fortunella margarita	Oval Kumquat	7 to 10	8	3	3	0	1		LMH	N	M	ANB
Fuchsia boliviana	Bolivian fuchsia	9 to 11	10	3.5	3	0	0	F	LMH	SN	M	ANB
Fuchsia corymbiflora	Peruvian Fuschia, Peruvian Berrybush, Vine fuchsia,	9 to 11	10	3.6	3	0	0		LMH	SN	M	ANB
Fuchsia denticulata		9 to 11	10	4	3	0	0		LMH	SN	M	ANB
Fuchsia fulgens		9 to 11	10	1.2	3	0	0		LMH	SN	M	ANB
Fuchsia hemsleyana		8 to 11	9	2	3	0	0	M	LMH	SN	M	ANB
Fuchsia microphylla		8 to 11	9	1.8	3	0	0		LMH	SN	M	ANB
Gaultheria adenothrix		8 to 11	9	0.3	3	0	4		LM	FS	M	AN
Gaultheria japonica	Creeping Snowberry	5 to 9	6	0.1	4	1	3	F	LM	S	MWe	AN
Gaultheria mucronata	Prickly heath	5 to 9	6	1.5	4	0	3		LM	SN	M	A
Gaultheria ovatifolia	Mountain Checkerberry, Western teaberry	5 to 9	6	0.2	3	0	3		LM	FS	M	AN
Gaultheria procumbens	Checkerberry, Eastern teaberry, Teaberry, Creeping Wintergreen	3 to 6	4	0.2	4	3	4	M	LM	FS	DM	AN

Growth: S = slow M = medium F = fast. **Soil:** L = light (sandy) M = medium H = heavy (clay)
pH: A = acid N = neutral B = basic (alkaline) **Light:** F = full shade S = semi-shade N = no shade. **Moisture:** D = dry M = Moist We = wet Wa = water

Scientific name	Common name	Zone							Soil	Shade	Moisture	Type
Gaultheria pyroloides		5 to 9	6	0.3	3	0	0		LM	S	M	AN
Gaylussacia dumosa	Dwarf Huckleberry	5 to 9	6	0.3	3	0	0		LM	SN	M	A
Gaylussacia frondosa	Dangleberry, Blue huckleberry	5 to 9	6	1.8	3	0	0		LMH	SN	DM	A
Gevuina avellana	Chilean Hazel	8 to 11	9	10	3	0	3	S	LMH	S	M	AN
Gymnanthemum amygdalinum	Bitterleaf	10 to 12	10	8	4	3	2	M	LMH	N	DM	ANB
Halimione portulacoides	Sea Purslane		0	0.8	3	0	0		LMH	SN	MWe	ANB
Hibiscus rosa-sinensis	Chinese Hibiscus, Shoeblackplant, Hawaiian Hibiscus, Tropical Hibiscus, China Rose, Rose-of-China, S	9 to 11	9	2.5	3	3	3	F	LMH	N	M	ANB
Hibiscus sinosyriacus	Rose Of Sharon	6 to 9	7	3	4	2	3	M	LMH	SN	M	ANB
Hippophae rhamnoides turkestanica	Sea Buckthorn	4 to 7	3	6	5	5	5	M	LMH	N	DMWe	ANB
Hydrangea macrophylla	French hydrangea , Florist's Hydrangea, Bigleaf Hydrangea	5 to 9	5	3	3	2	3	M	LMH	SN	M	ANB
Hydrangea serrata amagiana		5 to 9	6	2	4	0	2		LMH	SN	M	ANB
Hydrangea serrata thunbergii	Tea of heaven, Ama-tsja,	5 to 9	6	1.5	3	0	2		LMH	SN	M	ANB
Hylocereus megalanthus	Yellow Pitaya	10 to 12	10	2	4	0	0	F	LMH	N	DM	A
Hylocereus undatus	Dragon Fruit, Red Pitaya	10 to 12	10	4	4	0	2	F	LMH	SN	DM	AN
Juniperus communis nana	Juniper		2	9	3	3	4	S	LMH	SN	DM	ANB
Leptospermum scoparium	Tea Tree, Broom teatree, Manuka, New Zealand Tea Tree	8 to 11	8	5	3	0	3	M	LMH	N	DM	AN
Lespedeza bicolor	Lespedeza, Shrub lespedeza	4 to 8	5	3	3	0	4	M	LM	SN	DM	ANB
Lindera benzoin	Spice Bush, Northern spicebush, Bush Northern Spice	4 to 9	5	3	3	3	3	S	LMH	S	M	AN
Lippia graveolens	Mexican Oregano	9 to 12	10	2	4	0	0	F	LMH	N	DM	AN
Lonicera villosa solonis			2	0.8	3	0	0		LMH	N	M	ANB
Luma apiculata	Arrayan	8 to 11	9	6	3	0	3	M	LMH	N	M	ANB
Lycium carolinianum	Christmas Berry,	Carolina desert-thorn	7 to 10	8	1.5	3	2	3		LMH	N	M
Lycium europaeum	European tea-tree, Box thorn,	8 to 11	9	4	3	2	3		LMH	N	M	ANB
Lycium pallidum	Pale Wolfberry, Pale desert-thorn, Rabbit thorn	5 to 9	6	1.8	3	2	3		LMH	N	DM	ANB
Lycium ruthenicum		5 to 9	6	2	3	2	3		LMH	N	DM	ANB
Mahonia bealei	Beale's barberry, Leatherleaf Mahonia	5 to 8	6	2	3	2	0	S	LMH	FSN	M	ANB
Mahonia confusa		6 to 9	7	1.5	3	2	0		LMH	FS	M	ANB
Mahonia fortunei	Fortune's Mahonia	7 to 9	7	2	3	2	0	S	LMH	FSN	M	ANB
Mahonia fremontii	Mahonia, Fremont's mahonia	7 to 10	8	2.5	3	2	2	S	LMH	N	DM	ANB
Mahonia haematocarpa	Mexican Barberry, Red barberry	7 to 10	8	3.6	3	2	2		LMH	N	DM	ANB
Mahonia japonica		5 to 9	6	2	3	2	0		LMH	FSN	M	ANB
Mahonia lomariifolia	Chinese hollygrape	8 to 9	7	5	3	2	0	M	LMH	SN	M	ANB
Mahonia napaulensis		5 to 9	6	2.5	3	2	1		LMH	SN	M	ANB
Mahonia nervosa	Oregon Grape, Cascade barberry	5 to 9	6	0.6	3	2	3	S	LMH	FSN	DM	ANB
Mahonia nevinii	Nevin's barberry	7 to 10	8	2.4	3	2	2		LMH	N	DM	ANB
Mahonia pinnata	California Barberry, Wavyleaf barberry, Island barberry, Creeping Holly Grape	7 to 8	7	1.8	3	2	2	F	LMH	SN	M	ANB
Mahonia pumila	Dwarf Barberry	6 to 9	7	0.3	3	2	3	S	LM	SN	DM	ANB
Mahonia repens	Creeping Oregon Grape, Creeping barberry, Grape Oregon	4 to 8	6	0.3	3	3	4	S	LMH	SN	DM	ANB
Mahonia swaseyi	Texas Mahonia, Texas barberry	7 to 10	8	2.5	3	2	0		LMH	N	DM	ANB
Mahonia trifoliolata	Mexican Barberry, Algerita	6 to 9	7	2	3	2	4		LMH	N	DM	ANB
Mahonia x media		6 to 9	6	2	3	2	0		LMH	FSN	M	ANB
Malpighia emarginata	Acerola, Barbados Cherry	10 to 12	10	4	4	0	2	M	LMH	SN	M	AN
Malpighia glabra	Escobillo, Acerola	10 to 12	10	6	4	1	2	M	LMH	SN	M	AN
Manihot esculenta	Cassava, Tapioca Plant, Yuca	9 to 12	10	3	5	2	2	M	LMH	FSN	DM	ANB
Melianthus major	Honey Flower	7 to 10	8	3	3	1	1	M	LMH	SN	M	ANB
Melianthus minor	Honey Flower	7 to 10	8	2	3	0	0	M	LMH	SN	M	ANB
Mitchella repens	Partridge Berry	4 to 9	3	0.1	3	3	4	S	LM	SN	M	AN
Myrica californica	Californian Bayberry, California Wax Myrtle, California Barberry	7 to 11	7	4	3	1	3	M	LMH	SN	M	AN

Myrica heterophylla	Bayberry	5 to 9	6	3	3	2	3		LMH	SN	DM	ANB
Myrica pennsylvanica	Northern Bayberry		2	3	3	1	3		LMH	SN	DM	AN
Myrtus communis	Myrtle, Foxtail Myrtle	9 to 11	8	4.5	3	3	4	M	LMH	N	DM	ANB
Nypa fruticans	Nipa Palm, Mangrove Palm	11 to 12	10	5	3	2	4	M	LMH	N	MWeWa	ANB
Pandanus julianettii	Karuka	10 to 12	10	4	4	0	3	F	LM	SN	M	AN
Phyllanthus emblica	Emblica, Indian Gooseberry	10 to 12	10	15	3	5	2	S	LMH	N	DM	ANB
Pinus pumila	Dwarf Siberian Pine		1	3	3	2	3	S	LM	N	DM	AN
Pinus remota	Paper-Shell PiÒon	7 to 10	8	7	3	2	3		LM	N	DM	AN
Podocarpus nivalis	Alpine Totara	7 to 11	7	3	3	0	3	M	LMH	SN	M	AN
Prunus angustifolia watsonii	Sand Plum	5 to 9	6	3	4	1	1		LMH	SN	M	ANB
Prunus besseyi	Western Sand Cherry	3 to 6	3	1.2	4	1	2	M	LMH	SN	M	ANB
Prunus canescens	Greyleaf Cherry	5 to 9	6	3	3	1	2		LMH	SN	M	ANB
Prunus fruticosa	Mongolian Cherry, European dwarf cherry	4 to 8	4	1	3	1	1		LMH	N	DM	ANB
Prunus humilis	Bush Cherry	4 to 8	5	1.5	3	2	1		LMH	N	DM	ANB
Prunus incisa	Fuji Cherry	5 to 7	6	6	3	1	2	S	LMH	SN	M	ANB
Prunus japonica	Korean Cherry, Japanese bush cherry	4 to 8	4	1.5	3	3	1		LMH	SN	M	ANB
Prunus japonica nakai	Japanese Plum	4 to 8	4	0.5	3	3	1		LMH	SN	M	ANB
Prunus lusitanica	Portugal Laurel	6 to 9	7	6	3	1	5		LMH	SN	M	ANB
Prunus maritima	Beach Plum, Graves' plum	3 to 7	3	2.5	4	1	3		LMH	N	DM	ANB
Prunus orthosepala	Hybrid plum		0	6	3	1	1		LMH	N	M	ANB
Prunus pseudocerasus	Cambridge Cherry	5 to 9	6	3.5	4	1	1		LMH	SN	M	ANB
Prunus pumila susquehanae	Dwarf American Cherry		2	0.6	4	1	2		LMH	N	DM	ANB
Prunus spinosa	Sloe - Blackthorn	4 to 8	4	3	3	2	4	M	LMH	SN	M	ANB
Prunus tenella	Dwarf Russian Almond		2	0.8	3	1	3		LMH	S	DM	ANB
Prunus tomentosa	Nanking Cherry		2	1.5	3	1	1		LMH	SN	M	ANB
Prunus virginiana	Chokecherry, Western chokecherry, Black chokecherry		2	3.6	3	2	4	F	LMH	SN	M	ANB
Prunus virginiana demissa	Western Chokecherry		2	3.6	3	2	4		LMH	S	M	ANB
Prunus virginiana melanocarpa	Rocky Mountain Chokecherry		2	3.6	3	2	4		LMH	N	M	ANB
Psidium cattleianum	Strawberry Guava	9 to 12	10	6	3	0	3		LM	N	DM	ANB
Psidium cattleianum littorale	Yellow Strawberry Guava	9 to 11	10	6	3	0	3		LM	N	DM	ANB
Psoralea glandulosa	Culen	8 to 11	9	3	3	1	0		LMH	N	M	ANB
Pyronia veitchii		5 to 9	6	5	3	0	0		LMH	N	M	ANB
Quercus aucheri	Boz-Pirnal Oak	7 to 10	8	5	4	2	1	S	MH	SN	DM	ANB
Quercus coccifera	Kermes Oak	5 to 9	6	4	3	2	3		MH	SN	M	ANB
Quercus fruticosa		7 to 10	8	2	3	2	2		MH	N	M	ANB
Quercus gambelii	Shin Oak, Gambel oak, Rocky Mountain White Oak	4 to 8	4	4.5	3	2	3	S	MH	SN	DM	ANB
Quercus oblongifolia	Mexican Blue Oak	6 to 9	7	8	3	2	2		MH	SN	M	ANB
Quercus phillyreoides	Black ridge oak,	6 to 9	7	9	3	2	2	S	MH	SN	M	ANB
Rhus copallina	Dwarf Sumach, Winged sumac, Flameleaf Sumac, Winged Sumac, Shining Sumac	4 to 10	5	2	4	2	3	F	LMH	N	DM	ANB
Rhus glabra	Smooth Sumach	3 to 9	2	3	4	3	3	M	LMH	N	DM	ANB
Rhus trilobata	Skunk Bush, Basketbush, Squawbush, Three Leaf Sumac	4 to 6	3	1.8	4	2	3	M	LMH	N	DM	ANB
Rhus x pulvinata			2	3	4	2	2		LMH	N	DM	ANB
Ribes aciculare		3 to 7	3	1	3	0	0		LMH	SN	M	ANB
Ribes alpinum	Alpine Currant	2 to 7	2	1.2	3	0	4	M	LMH	SN	M	ANB
Ribes altissimum		5 to 9	6	3	3	0	0		LMH	SN	M	ANB
Ribes burejense	Bureja gooseberry,	4 to 8	5	1	4	0	0		LMH	SN	M	ANB
Ribes curvatum	Granite gooseberry	6 to 9	7	1	3	0	0		LMH	SN	M	ANB
Ribes cynosbati	Dogberry, Eastern prickly gooseberry		2	1.5	3	1	0		LMH	SN	M	ANB
Ribes divaricatum	Coastal Black Gooseberry, Spreading gooseberry, Parish's gooseberry, Straggly gooseberry	4 to 8	4	2.7	4	1	2		LMH	SN	M	ANB
Ribes fragrans		3 to 7	3	0.6	3	0	0		LMH	SN	M	ANB

Growth: S = slow M = medium F = fast. **Soil:** L = light (sandy) M = medium H = heavy (clay)

pH: A = acid N = neutral B = basic (alkaline) **Light:** F = full shade S = semi-shade N = no shade. **Moisture:** D = dry M = Moist We = wet Wa = water

Scientific name	Common name	Zone										
Ribes gayanum		7 to 10	8	1.5	3	0	0		LMH	SN	M	ANB
Ribes himalense		5 to 9	6	2	3	1	0		LMH	SN	M	ANB
Ribes hirtellum	Currant-Gooseberry, Hairystem gooseberry	4 to 8	4	1	3	0	0		LMH	N	M	ANB
Ribes horridum			0	1.5	3	0	0		LMH	SN	M	ANB
Ribes janczewskii			0	0	3	0	0		LMH	SN	M	ANB
Ribes lacustre	Prickly Blackcurrant, Prickly currant	4 to 8	4	1.5	3	1	2		LMH	SN	M	ANB
Ribes longiracemosum		5 to 9	6	3.5	3	0	0		LMH	SN	M	ANB
Ribes maximowiczii		5 to 9	6	2.7	4	0	0		LMH	SN	M	ANB
Ribes maximowiczii floribundum		5 to 9	6	2.7	4	0	0		LMH	SN	M	ANB
Ribes meyeri		6 to 9	7	1.5	3	0	0		LMH	SN	M	ANB
Ribes missouriense	Missouri Gooseberry	4 to 8	5	2	3	0	0		LMH	SN	M	ANB
Ribes montigenum	Gooseberry-Currant	5 to 9	6	0.8	3	0	0		LMH	N	M	ANB
Ribes odoratum	Buffalo Currant	4 to 8	5	2.5	4	1	0		LMH	SN	M	ANB
Ribes oxyacanthoides	American Mountain Gooseberry, Canadian gooseberry,		2	1.5	3	1	0		LMH	SN	M	
Ribes palczewskii			0	1.5	3	0	0		LMH	SN	M	ANB
Ribes petiolare	Wetern Blackcurrant	3 to 7	3	1.5	3	0	0		LMH	SN	M	ANB
Ribes petraeum	Rock Red Currant, Currant	5 to 9	6	1.8	3	0	0		LMH	SN	M	ANB
Ribes petraeum biebersteinii		5 to 9	6	1.5	3	0	0		LMH	SN	M	ANB
Ribes pinetorum	Orange Gooseberry	5 to 9	6	0	3	0	0		LMH	N	M	ANB
Ribes procumbens	Trailing red currant	3 to 7	3	0.2	4	0	0		LMH	SN	M	ANB
Ribes punctatum			0	0	3	0	0		LMH	SN	M	ANB
Ribes rotundifolium	Appalachian Gooseberry	5 to 9	6	1	3	1	0		LMH	SN	M	ANB
Ribes rubrum	Red Currant, Cultivated currant	4 to 8	5	1.2	4	1	2		LMH	SN	M	ANB
Ribes sachalinense			0	1	3	0	0		LMH	SN	M	ANB
Ribes sativum	Redcurrant	5 to 9	6	1	3	0	0		LMH	SN	M	ANB
Ribes triste	American Red Currant, Red currant		2	0.5	3	1	0		LMH	SN	M	ANB
Ribes warszewiczii	Downy currant	3 to 7	3	1.5	4	0	0		LMH	SN	M	ANB
Ribes x culverwellii	Jostaberry	5 to 9	6	1.8	5	0	0		LMH	SN	M	ANB
Rosa canina	Dog Rose	3 to 7	3	3	3	3	4	F	LMH	SN	MWe	ANB
Rosa corymbifera	Dog rose	5 to 9	6	3	3	1	0		LMH	SN	M	ANB
Rosa gigantea	Manipur Wild-Tea Rose	8 to 11	9	15	3	1	0		LMH	SN	M	ANB
Rosa nutkana	Nootka Rose, Bristly Nootka rose	4 to 8	4	2.7	3	2	4		LMH	SN	M	ANB
Rosa villosa	Apple Rose	4 to 8	5	1.8	4	1	1		LMH	SN	M	ANB
Rubus abbrevians	Vermont blackberry		0	0	3	0	1		LMH	SN	M	ANB
Rubus alleghaniensis	Alleghany Blackberry, Graves' blackberry	3 to 7	3	3	3	2	1	M	LMH	SN	M	ANB
Rubus almus	Mayes Dewberry, Garden dewberry	7 to 10	8	2	3	0	1		LMH	SN	M	ANB
Rubus amabilis		5 to 9	6	2	3	0	1		LMH	SN	M	ANB
Rubus biflorus			0	3.5	3	0	1		LMH	SN	M	ANB
Rubus corchorifolius	Fingerberry, Brombeere, Jute-leaved raspberry,	5 to 9	6	2.5	3	0	1		LMH	SN	M	ANB
Rubus crataegifolius	Korean raspberry	4 to 8	5	2.5	4	0	1		LMH	SN	M	ANB
Rubus cuneifolius	Sand Blackberry	5 to 9	6	0.5	3	0	1		LMH	SN	M	ANB
Rubus ellipticus	Golden Evergreen Raspberry, Yellow Himalayan raspberry	7 to 10	8	4.5	4	2	3		LMH	SN	M	ANB
Rubus flagellaris	Northern Dewberry	3 to 7	3	0.2	3	1	1		LMH	SN	M	ANB
Rubus fruticosus	Blackberry, Shrubby blackberry	5 to 9	6	3	5	3	2	F	LMH	FSN	M	ANB
Rubus geoides			0	0.6	4	0	1		LMH	SN	M	ANB
Rubus geophilus	Northern dewberry		0	0	3	0	1		LMH	SN	M	ANB
Rubus glaucus	Mora De Castilla, Andes berry	10 to 12	8	3	3	0	1		LMH	SN	M	ANB
Rubus gunnianus			0	0.2	3	0	1		LMH	SN	M	ANB
Rubus ichangensis		6 to 9	7	0.3	3	1	2		LMH	SN	M	ANB
Rubus idaeus	Raspberry, American red raspberry, Grayleaf red raspberry	4 to 7	3	2	5	3	2	M	LMH	SN	M	ANB
Rubus illecebrosus	Strawberry-Raspberry	4 to 8	5	0.6	3	0	3		LMH	SN	M	ANB
Rubus innominatus			0	3	3	0	1		LMH	SN	M	ANB